"It is only rarely that a theatergoer is overwhelmed by a performance. It's only rarely that the theater art provides these moments of mesmerism that make it art. Susan Merson's REFLECTIONS OF A CHINA DOLL is such an occasion."
CHARLOTTE OBSERVER

"REFLECTIONS OF A CHINA DOLL was an evening of fascinating theatre. A sparkling performance of wit and compassion."
NORTHERN ILLINOIS PRESS

In THE LOVES OF SHIRLEY ABRAMOWITZ, Merson, "…in authentic New York style … is messy but charming, volatile and articulate, enthusiastic and desperate. Susan Merson gives a virtuoso performance, filling the stage with a bunch of people one would easily recognize in Flatbush or the Village."
JERUSALEM POST

THE EXILE OF SARAH K
"Sarah K., played by her author Susan Merson, radiates a restless, erotic energy and a translucent vulnerability reminiscent of the silent film star Louise Brooks…When rehearsing the lines of her streetwalking come-on, about three young men in my row, grown oblivious to the boundary between reality and fiction, were about to leap over their chairs."
MOMENT MAGAZINE

In Sherry Glaser's FAMILY SECRETS
"Nothing like a one woman show to bring this year's Best Actress Citation. Merson played the quirk, cliché and reality of four characters. She changed costume and character right on stage, and she wasn't afraid to play the ache and edge of the personalities in the off Broadway comedy."
DETROIT NEWS

"The play is beautifully acted down to the last frigid moment. Susan Merson is completely convincing. Your response to her is liable to be complex; the same energy that makes her attractive is also what is ugly about her."
NEW JERSEY HOME NEWS

In CLARICE COHEN"S TRIBAL TALES OF LOVE
"What connects these "Tribal Tales"... is Merson's remarkable malleability as an actor. Her shifts from Clarice, a somewhat pretentious but indomitable born-again bohemian chanteuse who plays the Jewish retirement home circuit, to Betsy, a somewhat confused suburbanite, to Connie, the even more confused granddaughter of Clarice's lover, Ernie is the stuff of a true repertory style actor."
LOS ANGELES TIMES

"As Estelle, the murdered woman speaking to her granddaughter from the netherworld, Merson delivers a tour de force of passion energy and sadness. Estelle's speech is such a powerful expression of an old Jewish woman's abuse and loss and that these Tribal Tales cannot go much further. Indeed, Clarice reappears in silence...A quietly brilliant end to a deceptively complex work."
LOS ANGELES TIMES

# YOUR NAME HERE:

## An Actor and Writer's Guide to Solo Performance

# YOUR NAME HERE:
## An Actor and Writer's Guide to Solo Performance

By
# Susan Merson

# YOUR NAME HERE:
## An Actor and Writer's Guide to Solo Performance
©Susan Merson 2004

ISBN: 1-932993-03-7 (Print Book)
ISBN: 1-932993-04-5 (E-Book)

Library of Congress Number
LCCN: 2004098734

Edit, Cover and Interior Design
by Mystique Design and Editorial
Front Cover by Patrou Phelps
Interior Caricature by Sam Norkin

Published in 2004 by Star Publish

Printed in the United States of America

A Star Publish Book
http://starpublish.com
Nevada, U.S.A. and St. Croix, U.S.V.I.

# ACKNOWLEDGEMENTS

I thank the many inspirational writers in my life whose words have stayed with me and urged me forward. In particular, the words of William Carlos Williams, Franz Kafka, Colette, Anne Sexton and Willa Cather.

I thank the following friends, teachers and colleagues for all the many things they have contributed to this book whether they know it or not. In no particular order they are: Stephen Sachs and the Fountain Theatre Family, Evelyn Orbach and the JET Theatre Family, Curt Dempster and the Ensemble Studio Theatre Family, Neil Landau and the Goddard College MFA in Writing Family. Tony and Sofie Shultz, my very own.

And in particular, Jane Anderson, Ed Cohen, Janet Blake, Michael David, Dennis Drew, Gwen Feldman, Mel Gussow. Carolyn Howard-Johnson, Salome Jens, Kristie Leigh Maguire, Sam Norkin, Richard Panek, Stephanie Satie, Barbara Tarbuck, Randee Trabitz, Jule Selbo, Jan Quackenbush,

And to the Los Angeles Writers Bloc, then, now and forever.

"Morphing is an ongoing part of my life, it seems. It keeps me connected to myself and my world."

Stephanie Satie

# TABLE OF CONTENTS

Susan Merson as La Rousalka in
MUSIC HALL SIDELIGHTS
Credit: John Arnone

**FOREWORD: What's this book about and why should I read it?**

This book is about telling a story. The story can be yours. It can be someone else's. But, the book is about telling a story in the most concentrated fashion that you may have ever attempted. The effort will not be casual. The audacity needed is mighty.

You will ask an audience to sit in a room and listen to you talk in a concentrated way. You may even ask them to pay money to do so. Your proud parents will not be next to you grinning and affirming your cleverness. You will be on your own, lost in your own ether. There is nothing like it. You will be the "happy genius of your own household", as William Carlos Williams once said, and you will invite us in with your skill, passion and deep intention.

In these chapters, I have laid out six different ways of creating a solo play. I include exercises for you to help define your work. I ask you to think long and hard about the undertaking. At the end of the book, you will have an overview of one person's technique of creating solo pieces for the stage. There will be observations on acting style, writing choices and producing tips.

I have organized the book chronologically. I begin with the first piece I created and move through time with you, allowing you to see how time itself mellowed both my subject matter and the way in which the pieces came together. This is not primarily a reference book. It is a storybook. The book will tell you the story of a storyteller creating people and places for audiences. My work and observations change with the years. I hope the progression from one stage to the next is as instructive as finding the exact page where I address the interpretation of multiple characters in various voices.

Of all the different kinds of performing I have done, solo performing allows me to be at my most relaxed and most unique. Franz Kafka said, "All art is a form of prayer". And so it is, especially with solo performing. The solo performer is quiet within and open to the energy that flows through her. Her movements and choices are streams of clear thought.

Solo performance is meditation at its highest. When everything works, the Performer disappears, and the heightened Storyteller appears.

Susan Merson as Ernie in
CLARICE COHEN'S TRIBAL TALES OF LOVE
Photo by Barbara Bloom

**INTRODUCTION: Why go it alone? The compelling reason to proceed. The generative vs. the interpretative artist**

"Passion is the very fact of God in Man"—Paddy Chayefsky

PASSIONATE CONNECTION
I have a passion for the theatre. I love the simple exchange of people sitting in a room together, breathing the same air and experiencing the same story as it enters and transforms the space between them. I have learned more in small black box theatres in crummy neighborhoods, onstage and off, than in the fancy show palaces uptown. The uptown spots thrill and overwhelm me, but the small space, where the actor must be still and simple to let the tale emerge, is the place where the real magic happens for me.

I love language. I love ritual. I love danger. I love the drive toward survival. I even love that for most people in this country the "theatre" doesn't exist. There is a dinosaur element to this ancient craft that many in this high tech, cyber world can connect with no longer. It's like an unknown river of fiery lava that flows beneath the cement and freeways of our consciousness these days. In most places in America, it's a secret. There are weary practitioners who barely earn a living but still they return, revitalized by the truth of it. There is a primal call and though it's a call many do not understand, I have come to terms with the fact that there is value in being a person of the theatre. To me, a person in the theatre must be a person with a passionate voice; ready to speak the truth in every piece of work they create.

In my years of teaching, performing, writing and producing, I have noted a real change. Coming of age in the emotive, sexy and overblown 1960's, I was surrounded with people who couldn't wait to spill their heart, toot their own horns and preach their political doctrine. We

9

were all about encounter groups and "happenings" and Esalen sensitivity training and "group grope" sessions in theatre school. Mind and body were assailed with gusts of wind from ridiculously open doorways. Much good came from this time. Some damage, too. But the essential nature of this time was one of experimentation and claiming the right to a voice. Feminism—good! Racism—bad! Free love—good! Military-industrial complex—bad. It was a time of "my country right or wrong" for some and "my own thing—right or wrong" for others.

Then the Viet Nam War was over. And cynicism borne of defeat and then Watergate and greed borne of Reaganism swept the country and young people learned to shut up and down and don a three-piece suit. And then, AIDS hit and not only were doors shut tight, but legs were crossed once again, breasts were buttoned behind punk armor and necks that once sported love beads now sported dog collars.

I remember teaching a workshop in the early 1990's where a young woman wrote a play about relationship and her heroes never touched, never alluded to sexuality and never even quivered. Her version of love was whining on a black telephone for 45 minutes to a closeted gay boy who shaved his legs as he talked to her. Here lies passion, said she. The vicarious thought of being together and shedding skin— quite literally—to come closer.

Interesting, I thought. But what of poetry? What of passion? What of connection? I suppose the play was illustrative of all three by the lack of all three but it was troubling to me as an educator and playwright. How could this talented young woman speak of what held her hostage? How could she write about why she never removed her glasses or leather vest or never hazarded a connection on any level with a real person until after she received a clean AIDS test certificate and at least three clearances from a dating service. Her case was extreme perhaps but I have long pondered the difference between constipation and style and now am willing to state that what passed for style in this young artist was truly a constipation of the spirit.

Shakespeare might say, "A rose by any other name might smell as sweet". I might look at the symbolic rather than the actual in this young person's run at relationship in the new millennium. But I pause.

I want to put in a vote for old fashioned passionate commitment, connection and the guts to take a stand emotionally, artistically and even politically, if the reader acknowledges the connection between all three states of being. This is exactly what a solo performer does.

Solo performers connect with their passion and have the guts to take the full responsibility of telling their story to the world. They are the generative artists. Of course, one can be an artist with an independent and defined voice, even as an interpretative artist.

## INTERPRETATIVE VS. GENERATIVE ARTIST

But what is the difference between an interpretative and generative artist? Let's talk about being the megaphone rather than the voice that comes through it. That is, being an interpretative artist rather than a generative one. The interpretative artist is one that takes an existing idea and expresses it through the medium of his/her own consciousness, physicality and experience. This is an art in itself. Each actor comes to a role with different experience. Therefore, each actor portrays a role differently. But, an actor who speaks someone else's words exclusively remains a tool of the writer, delivering someone else' message.

Most actor training focuses on simplifying and clearing out thought, action and deed so that one can accept and become "part of" the character being portrayed. Interpretative artists, like actors, do have a voice through the openness of the body or the "actor's instrument". The actor becomes the structure within which the voice of the writer and the vision of the director resonate. They have a voice by virtue of the kind of work they choose to perform. Every choice has its reasons and every reason adds up to an actor's statement. The interpretative artist is the messenger. The interpretative artist speaks elegantly, but speaks others words.

Now let us come to the generative artist. She is the one who starts from scratch and delivers her own voice into the world. She does the alchemy, spins the gold and delivers it to marketplace.

## MAKING THE COMMITMENT

As a young artist, still a teenager, I remember coming across this quote by Andre Gide, which stopped me, cold. I paraphrase it here:

> "Look for your own," Gide said. "Do not do what someone else can do as well as you. Do not say, do not feel, and do not think what someone else can say, feel or think as well as you.

Look for your own. And out of yourself create. You are the most irreplaceable of beings."

The idea that each one of us has something unique, some cellular peculiarity that is important for the balance of the universe, gives us each a special position, a "saved space" for whatever it is we are going to bring into the world. Indeed, it lays our obligations clearly before us. We each have something to give and the job is to find it, hone it and toss it into the soup. To paraphrase Delmore Schwartz: "our dreams create responsibility".

## SPEAKING THE TRUTH, CREATING THE WORLD

As a teenager, I remember picking up The Diary of Anne Frank. I had already played Anne a few times as young girl but when I started to read the diary this second time, as a committed young artist, I learned something new. It wasn't that Anne's observations of the world were so extraordinary. All young girls felt those things. No. It was that they were so deeply true. True to her character, her time and her situation, despite the madness and tragedy that surrounded her. Her truth, which included not only the insights but the resonance from the world from which she spoke to us, gave us a larger sense of truth.

"I still believe that people are really good at heart," says 16-year-old Anne. She speaks these words of innocence from a hidden garret while the world is turning upside down. Now her truth is greater than her insight. Now we know who she is. A young girl, fierce with innocence. And we are moved that her truth remains so steadfast and piercing as we read not only her words but also her world. She has spoken in a way that no one else could have. She becomes Gide's "most irreplaceable of beings".

That is exactly what the successful solo artist does. She speaks the truth from her heart against the backdrop of a clear and present World.

So, I read Anne Frank's words and her world at the same time. And everything she said resonated differently because I understood her emotion and realized that it was made more brilliant and polished by the world from which it emerged. The world itself was the antagonist of her story. The world gave her story conflict and that conflict is what honed the detail and pierced the veil of mediocrity. Her small observations became profound because her words reverberated showing us what was underneath and all around them.

12

Anne Frank taught me to speak the truth, from my world, as an artist. She taught me that the universal was in the specific. She did not describe my world. She described hers and the light with which she illuminated her experience shot right through time and space and spoke to me in my world at my time. How could this be so?

It is so because the artist slows us right down. Our everyday lives move quickly. They zap from encounter to encounter, image to undigested image, and exchange to spontaneous exchange. But what does the artist do for us? The artist isolates, polishes and shines the detail that refracts light into our own experience.

When Anne speaks of her love for Peter, she speaks of all our first lovers. When she strives to keep her faith in the world, we recognize our own basic optimism borne of conscience and our own struggle to believe, so we can go on living.

As solo artists, we have our own true voice and the world from which we speak. These two elements are in sharp contrast to each other and they are what create the dynamic of a dramatic solo play. How the Storyteller emerges from and fights with the elements of her World determines the pitch of conflict, the level of inherent debate in the play. The higher the level of debate, the higher the conflict, and the hotter the heat—the more drama is created.

QUESTIONS TO PONDER:
What do you know, feel or think that no one else does? OK. A tough one to start with but give it a try.
What is the quiet voice inside of you that needs to be heard?
How do you process the world on your own terms? What is your digestive mechanism? What lenses shape your view?
How do you define your world—the one from which you are writing?
What are your own terms?
The rhythm of your language?
The things you observe?
The world you come from?
What makes your story come from you?
Why do you need to tell it and why do we need to hear it?

**NOTES:**

Susan Merson as Girl in REFLECTIONS OF A CHINA DOLL
Credit: Leah Posluns Theatre

# I: "REFLECTIONS OF A CHINA DOLL"- THE AUTOBIOGRAPHICAL PIECE: Finding Your Unique Voice

As a young actor in New York, I was lucky enough to appear in and help create a long running Off-Broadway hit. In over eight hundred performances, I said the same words; made the same moves, and every night interacted with a new audience bringing their sensibilities and reactions to the work. This long run became like a meditation. I was able to lose myself and truly time travel through the movements that became ritualized after a year or so. The language that came from my mouth was more like song than speech.

Every night I sat in a little cubicle on the stage of the Chelsea Westside Theatre bouncing to music that had become a part of my body as an original member of the longest running Off Broadway non-musical play in history, VANITIES by Jack Heifner. I could even feel myself leaving my body and traveling out into the cosmos as the movements and sounds supported me. There were times that this was a deeply unfettered experience, feeling so much a part of a moment that I ceased to exist as separate from it. I was the moment. No duality. All I needed to do was repeat the words, the mantra, do the movements, the Dance, and I would be free to travel the Heavens. Heady stuff, indeed, but as real as taking the subway to the theatre every night or drinking champagne cocktails at Charlie's restaurant after the show.

This searing understanding of what allowed us to connect with the larger force—whatever we want to call it—taught me the power of ritual and the power of Art. But with this unity came chaos as well.

Sitting in front of people, clothed and unclothed, every night for three years while people stared at my every move began to give me a physical sensation of "eye burn". My skin literally felt blistered, singed by the eyes of people staring at me, naked and dolled up, night after night.

Director Garland Wright had set the play up as a voyeuristic hot box. We, the three actresses, posed between acts. We stared haughtily into space; we placed our bodies into the river of curiosity that all people seem to have about themselves. We, the actresses, were the audience looking at us looking at them.

There were powerful aspects to this work. We owned the energy of the space. It was ours. The three of us together—Jane Galloway, Kathy Bates and I—were driven by Jack's words and Garland's vision, draped in the clothes designed by David James and a set designed by John Arnone. We were the personification of all the artists as we channeled the visions of all these men, but we were not ourselves. We were representations of others.

When the play worked, it was like prayer. When we were out of sync with each other, it was like bad sex with an abusive hooker. The show became like a whining car trying to find the spark to get the thing going. The tensions that we each ingested, very soon created too much distaff between us. Fights broke out. Late night drama ensued after the audience was gone. Accusations and misunderstandings flew. Lots of opinions and value judgments started crowding us all out of the dressing room as the show got hotter and hotter and everyone got greedier and greedier for some kind of fame or recognition. There was no pleasing anyone, least of all ourselves. I felt myself being swallowed completely by everyone else's vision of who and what I should be. I needed to get back in touch with who I was as an artist—not as a character, not as someone else's minion.

I am reminded of the story of actor Lee. J. Cobb who lost his center as he portrayed Willie Loman in the original production of DEATH OF A SALESMAN by Arthur Miller. As Cobb became closer and closer to the realization of Willie, he forgot who he was, as an artist and as a man. Too much intimacy, even for such an ecstatic effort.

Impressed by the vision of Ensemble Studio Theatre founder and Artistic Director Curt Dempster, I realized that I was losing myself, as I became increasingly a part of the VANITIES maelstrom. Dempster had created a theatre where actors were encouraged to develop their own work, and their own voices. He created a theater space where member artists could come at any time and put up a piece of their own choosing and creation. The cost to the artist was zero dollars. A good friend was a member there and she and Curt introduced me to the real possibility of producing my own work.

At the same time, I began to distrust the call and response I was experiencing onstage in VANITIES. The vagaries of success were pressuring everyone in this little hit of a show and we began to splinter. We lost the trust so necessary in an ensemble piece. I didn't want to return to my body and the real world after a performance. It was too painful. I needed to move forward as an artist but was fearful of losing myself in a puddle of political intrigues. I was pushed to examine other options but not sure what they were.

At about the same time that the long run performing in VANITIES was getting difficult, I met a young journalist, Diana K. Bletter, who began to question me about my own process as an artist. How had I arrived at this point in my career? How had I moved from the Midwest, gotten involved in a public and commercial success in the theatre and did I still have a strong sense of myself? She wanted me to define some of the moments that had gotten me from there to New York and to share them with her and the readers of Lilith Magazine, a Feminist Jewish monthly, where she was working.

A COMPELLING REASON

As our friendship grew, Diana challenged me to define my journey for her readers. I chose the moments that I knew were shifts in awareness. I did this partly to satisfy her questions and partly to figure out the answers for myself. I chose to explore the moments when I learned a lesson that moved me ahead, even if I could not exactly articulate the lesson. But, I was still tentative. I was not committed to this work. I had no real, driving need to tell my story.

At age 28, I was leaving the sphere of family and home and embracing my new life as a single woman, a committed artist in an adversarial metropolitan city. I fumbled with a direction for a few more months and showed the stories to another friend, Paul Cooper, who helped me to edit them but still they had no urgency as far as I was concerned.

And, then, my mother attempted suicide for the first time.

My work became my lifeline. It was something I could hold onto. And I had to do it.

My mother had always been the solid center of my life. When she began to lose her grip, it necessarily forced me to look at where I came from and where I was going. I had to ask these questions and come up with answers or I would drown.

QUESTIONS TO PONDER:
Why write this story now?
What compelling reason is pushing you forward?
Does it carry enough heat to ignite a full play? A short story?
How does this compelling reason shape the play you envision?

## YOUR STORY ARC

One is counseled to write what one knows, but even at that time I realized what I knew might not have amounted to much and even if it did, was there anyone who would be interested? So, I began the process by listening to Diana's questions. Where were the turning points in my artistic life so far? Who had been the impetus for these turning points? How did these turning points relate to each other? If these turning points were clear, coming from a particular world, could they be seen as universal? Were my questions passionate enough to allow other people to ask them as well?

## HOW DO YOU GET THERE? BUILDING THE STORY FROM THE BASICS

These questions were most important to me as I began my writing journey. But, how will you get there? Let's start slow and steady. You may find this section elementary and it is meant to be. We are starting once again from a place of knowing nothing. And we will see if we really have a story to tell.

## BUY A JOURNAL AND A BRAND NEW PENCIL

The first step is defining the specifics. Take a look at your life and start a personal journal. You need to start observing yourself and see what themes begin to emerge. Find some paper right now. Nothing fancy. An old notebook or the back of a script will do. No one will see these scribblings. They are all yours.

## BLURT BLURT BLURT

Begin to think about moments that affected you deeply in your life and, using the first person, begin to write these stories down. Just as simply as that. Don't think too much. Just find the first phrase—like once upon a time—and move on from there. Enjoy the way the pencil moves across the page. It's part of the fun.

each room. Someone crying? An animal barking or purring? Laughter? Whispering? Screaming? Boring conversation? Connect that sound with a story, an event that happened in that room. Write that event down.

>FOR INSTANCE:
>ROOM: KITCHEN
>SOUND: water running
>MEMORY: A bloody cut from a kitchen knife rendered my 15-year-old brother speechless. Did he do it on purpose?
>
>ROOM: DINING ROOM
>SOUND: the tinkle of china cups in the mahogany cabinet
>MEMORY: My father had sat there for days saying nothing. Only the sound of the tinkling china signaled when he adjusted his position or got up to pace.
>
>ROOM: DEN
>SOUND: My Dad snoring and the sound of the football game
>MEMORY: sleeping on my daddy's stomach as he snored, feeling like I was sleeping in a rowboat
>
>ROOM: LIVING ROOM
>SOUND: The dog panting and crying
>MEMORY: The dog suffered terribly from distemper and my tough father held him so tenderly as he swabbed the animal's nose and spoke to him in a mixture of Yiddish and Greek.

Then, place yourself in the room next to the one that has an event happening, overhear the conversations, and see if it has anything to do with you. Is there anything you discover that you didn't already know about your family, the people in the rooms, the memories that still live there? Observe with all five senses in mind. Sight, touch, smell, hearing and taste.

>EXAMPLES:
>I sit in the kitchen and listen to my parents argue about whether I am smart enough to make it in the private school nearby. I stare (SEE) at the kitchen tile

chattering like chilly teeth, mocking me and can HEAR the sound of my childhood record Billy and the Bat. "You're nothing but a nothing," sings the Bat to Billy. I TASTE the remnants of the bread and butter I shouldn't have eaten because I'm on a diet yet again and SMELL the greasy gravy from the pot roast that spilled all over the stove. I try to wipe it off but it FEELS like an invisible coating that will never let me get to what is underneath.

Finish this paragraph? Remember to add the five senses.

I lay awake in bed, listen to my sister weep, and hear the sound of three doors slamming one after the other.

_____
_____
_____
_____
_____

From this kind of work you can begin to explore the richness of your own life story. Dig around and see what happens. Go deeper and spend much longer with the exercise than I have here, and keep coming back to it. It is the meat of your personal tale.

FIND ACTIONS
Go back through your vignettes and see if you can define each paragraph with an action word. Just do it. Know that this will come in handy later when you are building the arc of your story, and the arc of your play.

FIND THEMES
Are any emerging? What do you tend to write about? Eating? Making love? Hiding? Hoping?

NOW, YOUR VOICE
Let the stories emerge from your unconscious and find their way onto the page. Take as long as you need but not longer than a week. Try not to diffuse your energy by over thinking at this stage of the work. Keep going and throw something into the pot. Anything will do. Let your life become stories. Write them down and offer them up.

Subtitle each story with an action word. Or see if you can finish the sentence "This is a story about _____", for each of the stories you have. Notice if the main character is active or passive. If the event is internal (intellectual/passive) or external, (usually more actable/active and dramatic).

## WHAT DO YOU SOUND LIKE?
Then, all by yourself, get a small tape recorder and read the stories aloud. You can look in the mirror while you are reading. That is sometimes informative, sometimes scary. When you start looking bored to yourself, you're probably boring the folks who are watching you. Begin to cultivate the ability to be connected to the story you are telling but aware of the way in which you are telling it. Whose voice is coming from you? Your childhood voice? The voice of your best friend? Your favorite monster? Who is narrating your story?

## NOTICE BUT REMAIN ALOOF
This is a very tricky technique. It can be deadly for an actor to begin looking or listening to himself while performing. This is certainly true in a play. However, in a situation like this where you are playing yourself, you become more a stand up performer than an actor. What is needed here is a consciousness of your affect with out a self-consciousness that will inhibit your delivery. This is why language becomes so important. If you do not have a character to disappear into, then you can meld with the language itself, the rhythms, the jigs and jogs of the words as they trip off your tongue. Try rhyming or rapping for your story? What happens then? No judgment, just jive.

## WHERE IN MY BODY DOES THIS STORY RESIDE?
Begin to develop the ability to hear your voice physically. Where does it sit in your head, your throat? Does it feel good to speak these words? Do they come out easily? Do they fit your own physical rhythms? As you speak the words, do they have physicality to them that you can lean into as a performer? Do you get a cramp? Or give yourself a headache? Note your reactions to yourself.

## THE RESPITE
Stop already. Phew. That's over. If you need a break now, put down the tape recorder and your notebook and go for a run or a swim or do anything that doesn't include major cogitation. Screaming is fine. Cleanse your palate and forget about all the things you have just revealed in your work. No one saw you except you. You are still safe.

## THE RETURN
Next night, or whenever it seems right, get into the bath tub with lots of bubbles or somewhere you find equally relaxing, set up your tape recorder and listen to yourself reading these stories. Remember if you do it in the bathroom that the echo will make your voice sound positively wonderful!

What do you notice? Do the stories move fast enough for you to remain interested? How does your voice sound? Are you putting yourself to sleep? Are there any jokes? Too many?

This secret exercise of being your own audience first can be a sobering experience. We are always our own toughest critics. Know that you are absolutely, positively at least fifty percent better sounding than you think. Give yourself several breaks. Then, straighten up, dry off and take a walk. Good for you. You found some things. Maybe, you learned a few things.

## FIND THE UNIVERSAL
Think about what you heard and now—be tough on yourself. Know that you are brave and know that if we are to be solo performers then we must have the courage and the confidence in our voices as actors and writers. Do these stories need to be in the world?
Are these stories universal and distanced enough to communicate their essence to the reader? That means that the central core is about a specific discovery that is placed before the viewer. It is placed there for the audience to decide how THEY feel about it. Be careful that you write these stories allowing the audience room to respond from their experience not yours. Show them yourself rather then tell them about yourself. Here's where the specific of the five senses come in.

TAKE A DISPASSIONATE RETURN to the work you have created. Notice areas where you are truly committed to what you are saying. Note these passionate moments, then go back, and see if you can bring the same commitment to every part of your story. Whittle it down so the passionate moments, your passionate voice, emerges as an actor and a writer. Notice the moments when you or your main character is actually DOING something. Remember you must act these stories and TO ACT is TO DO. So, find the active passages and make them passionate.

## AND AGAIN PLEASE
Listen and listen again. Write and write again.

Keep writing, Keep listening and eventually you will hear your truest, most active and most passionate voice speaking.

This may take a long time or just a few days. Don't rush your rhythm. Give yourself the luxury of a "shitty first draft" as writer Anne Lamott calls it. Face it. You're new at this. You may have too much. Fine. You'll cut it later.

BE THE CREATOR. DECIDE ON LIFE AND DEATH
Give your stories the oxygen test. Do they really demand that they receive oxygen and live? OK. Then they stay in. Be nice to your emerging voice—voices—but be firm as well. Make them tell the truth. Make them succinct and only write what you absolutely must.

FIND A PLACE THAT YOU CAN LIVE WITH
When you have a basic draft, gather some good friends and ask them if they will sit and listen to you. Tell them the rules. They must applaud your effort. They must encourage you to keep writing and they must tell you what they really liked. You will know what they did not like by the way they pay attention or not. Do it.

BREATHE.
OK. Not so bad. Your friends are still talking to you. Now, get a hot fudge sundae together and put your script away for at least a week.

REPOSE
Congratulations. You have introduced your voice to the world. Now you can analyze the responses, both your own and that of your audience. Decide whether you want to proceed or if you have finished the project. Anything you decide is just fine. So much of our work is process rather than product.

GET OVER THE NEED FOR A RESULT RIGHT NOW
The mere act of getting this far, of making a commitment to your voice and your stories has a real effect in the world. You are participating in the exchange of knowledge and the drive for understanding that everyone shares. This is no small accomplishment. Many have not dared to formalize their desire to stake a claim to a place on the planet. Well done.

If you want to stop here, you have still accomplished much. If you feel you have more work to do, then approach it with strength and certainty that you have more to learn and more to offer. Be willing now to look at the work in a more technical light.

## THE RETURN

THE NEXT STEP
Let's assume that each story has a beginning, middle and end. Each story has a motor. Find the motor. What is the central event that drives your story? This is a story about_____? Make a list of the events of each story. Look at them and see if you can see an arc emerging, a pattern? Is each story telling us something new?

Once you know what your motor is you may find that it's sluggish here and there. Perhaps the stories don't go deep enough. Or they go too deep for the affect you are after. Do you tell us too much?

REGROUP
When you are ready to go back to your work, play with rhythm in your story. Short sentences. Long words. Short words. Long sentences. Alliterations? Onomatopoeia? See how these technical language tricks can affect the way in which people hear your story. How can the words themselves keep the listener interested? Find writers that play with language to define themselves. How about Grace Paley? Eminem? Faulkner?

Examine your first story and see if that covers the landscape of your intent. If not, decide where you are missing an element and add a new story or expand an existing one to create a beginning, middle and an end to the arc that will become your play. The movement from the beginning, through the middle and to a satisfying end is your story arc.

WHAT IS YOUR STORY ARC? YOUR CENTRAL IMAGE?
Identify for yourself those specific events in your life that, when added together, create the story arc of a character. Is your play about coming of age? Is it about learning how to love? About over coming a particular challenge?

Once you know what your story wants to say you will know which events to choose. In movie lingo, this is called your HOOK. You should be able to fill in the blanks.

This is a story about_____(something active/ verb)_____.

The building blocks of this personal story are carefully chosen from my life and they are_____.

Choose events in which you realized something new and surprising. Choose odd events that taught you a standard lesson or standard events that taught you an odd lesson. Each event contributes to an overall theme.

For my story arc in CHINA DOLL, I began with and ended with my mother. From my most secure memory to my scariest memory. I realized that what I received from my mother was a sense of community that, for better or worse, sustained me and took me as its own even if I rejected it. So, my story started in the synagogue as a child playing with the fringe of my father's prayer shawl and snuggling into the luxurious sensuality of my mother's mink coat and the scent of middle class success, Arpege perfume.

In this selection from REFLECTIONS OF A CHINA DOLL, I describe the world that surrounds me in sensual terms, and place myself in its secure and smug center as a contented and bored five-year-old child. Note the language and how it works with or against the character of a five-year-old:

> It is Saturday morning and I am lost in a sea of fringe. [1] Bodies
> swaying and bobbing around me. But mostly,
> safely hidden am I, couched next to my Daddy's smell of Old
> Spice
> and the feel of fringe everywhere and forever.
> My fingers reach out to tangle it, then
> to disentangle it from myself, and to
> braid the strings that fall and give me
> strands of white hair long before I am grown. [2]

> The service is moving along now and I settle down into my
> hard backed, soft cushioned mahogany seat.

> BARUCH ATA ADOSHEM—ELOKEHENU MELECH
> HAOLAM [3]

*see page 42 for footnotes

My eyes wander [4]as I listen to the drone of the tefilla
the lethargic congregational responses
and the whining supplication of the cantor
and before I know it I am whisked away into sleep.

Gently, I am wrapped and cradled in a ladies fur coat
who is seated next to me. She has let my head droop on her
shoulder and now has swaddled me in mink to snuggle in for
the rest of the service.

My cheeks caressed by cashmere and fur,
my nose breathing in the heady fumes of Arpege.[5]
One hand still clutching my Daddy's tzittzit.
Little stubby fingers measuring themselves against the graceful
strands of linen snow.

> THE CHILD DRIFTS OFF TO
> SLEEP, SHE SITS UP SUDDENLY
> AND SINGS LOUDLY.

> ADON OLAM ASHER MOLACH. BETER IM CHAL
> YETSEER NEEVRA.[6]

I am awake! My nose picks up the sniff of marble cake and
éclairs coming from the social hall. Ah Kiddush! Ah cookies
and cakelets!

ACTING CHOICES
In this piece, I had the responsibility as an actress to create my
environment as well as the character. My one chair was a trusty prop.
My feet curled under me and dangled off the floor. Presto, I am three
feet tall. I look up and out and my gaze delineates the range and
dimension of the synagogue. My eyes widen, the limbs become gangly
and awkward and the words become like candy in my mouth, sliding
around and making me silly, sleepy, secretive and hyperactive all at
once. A five-year-old but with the language of an adult.

LIP CANDY
Language itself was the tool I began to experiment with in CHINA
DOLL. I suggest you play with it as you develop your own pieces. I
often will choose elevated language and ask that a down to earth
character speak it. What results is a natural tension between language
and character.

*see page 42 for footnotes

In solo performing, I have found that this extra dynamic creates a complexity that draws the viewer in and encourages them to see past both the words and the actions to a larger more universal message. Performing any poetic language can be tough if the specific truth of the character is missing. Make sure to know the person who is speaking the words—your character. The words do not function as direct information for character, as they might in a realistic, kitchen sink drama. Instead, the life of the character exists as a heart beat below the language that moves above it like an inexorable river. Think of Shakespeare and how the best performers use the "truth" of their characters to inform the energy of the language. When it works it can be wonderful.

So, the first piece established the child's most secure secret world. Tucked in between her parents, wrapped in luxury and bathed in the sounds of a tradition that had seen an entire people through slavery and into the Promised Land. This kid was well taken care of.

ESTABLISHING CONTEXT
But, I wanted to expand her world before I shattered it in the second act. I needed to establish a larger context for her life. I also wanted to expand her world by introducing more voices, more people who surround and support her. And from an acting point of view, I would have the opportunity to portray an entire room of screaming relatives. It was great fun. Here is the introduction to the family.

> Beside the quilted sofa, on the floor in the corner, there was a flat gray place that smelled a bit of dust but more of furniture polish. A long slit of a window came down and fit nicely under my eight-year-old elbows. My fingers played with the black iron window turners and my forearms delighted in the coolness of the marble sill. From this slice in the front side of our house I could look out and see the cement slab front porch and tell from the movement of the green shrubs just who was about to step up and enter.[7]

> My Daddy was all clean in his all day white shirt as he came forward to answer the door, the neck open now, but the collar still stiff. His cheek just rough enough to give me a rouge with a rub-dub of his cheek to mine. He answered the door because my Mom was still upstairs dressing and my brother

*see page 42 for footnotes

Richard was taking out the garbage and my sister Barbara was silently sifting Comet onto the porcelain of the kitchen sink.[8]

Then all of a sudden, crashing into the stillness, I heard: "OH HELLOOOO LOOOOOU!"

A cacophony of sound. Cackles and yells. Giggles from mid-forties matrons and all the aunts swept into the living room covering my Daddy with their careful juicy kisses.

"Esther, is that you?" called my mom from upstairs.

"Yes, Shula. Get down here! We're ready to start the family club meeting. Rose, you be the recording secretary, Leonard, sit here with Batya and stop teasing Lou. Herschel get the finance report ready and SHULA!!!! COME DOWNSTAIRS ALREADY! WE'RE READY TO START THE FAMILY CLUB MEETING!"

"Alright, Esther! I'm here. Stop shrying!"

"Kine hora! You loooook BEEE YOOOTIFULLLL! New dress?"

"Saks", says my Mom.

"Not paid for," says my Dad.

"Rose!" Read the letter from Sid in Yisroel!"[9]

"E-N-C-Y-C-L-O-P-E-DIA"

I had heard it all before and was content to nestle near the rhythms of my families club meeting but I'd rather make my own music.[10]

"E-n-c-y-c—"

"Pssst! Mamale! Vas mach tzu?" whispered my Uncle Leonard to me under the din, his twinkly blue eyes giggling through big black glasses.

"I'm singing."

"Oh," says Leonard, long and low. "I've got a better song for you. It goes... MADEL MADEL, BISMEER GEFELN."

"Madel, madel, bismeer she fell in."

"Good. Ich vil der kafen, a buncke reln."

"Ich vil der cave man..."

"...Yes, a bunchke reln. Zog der hasidl, bim bam."

"Zog der hasidl, bimbam!" I sang triumphantly to my Uncle's delight.

*see page 43 for footnotes

"LEONARD!" Esther is shrying. "You're teaching the baby dirty songs!"

"Which one, Leonard!" Herschel cries. "Oh, what are you talking? That's not dirty!"

"Leonard! Esther! Herschel!" screams my mother. "If you're going to teach the baby songs, teach her some of the songs that we used to sing as children. What did Tateh used to sing?"

"I remember," says Rose the matriarch. "Listen, mamale, when we were children every Friday night after Shabbos dinner we would sit around the table and sing the zmirot, the shabbos songs under the strict conductorship of Tateh's right forefinger. The first song we always sang was… What was it?"

"Zingche alle yidelach, dem neegan , dem nayim, dem neegan, dem nayim."

"I'll sing the high part," says Esther.

"Oh, you always sing flat," says my Mom.

"I do not! Tateh always said I had a lovely voice!"[11]

Their Tateh. My Zedah had been ninety when he stepped onto an airplane with tailor scissors and a bottle of whiskey tucked inside his jacket like a bulletproof vest. He had gone to Israel to die under an olive tree with the juice of a Jaffa orange trickling down his throat, followed by a chaser from the Jordan River. And that's where he's buried. He did that.[12]

"Oy," says Rose. "Just like when we were children. Almost the full choir, except for Sonia Sophia, of course and Sid."

Their sister, Sonia Sophia had strayed from the family fold, moved to New York, married a goy and by all family accounts still couldn't cook a decent dinner. I'd only met my Uncle Sid one time when he had been to visit from Israel. They were all very far away but they did complete the family picture.

"Ah," says Rose. "But the best song of all, mamale, was the song that Mother used to sing. She would sing this song, Mamale and cry and cry.

Oifen pripichik, brent a firereh
Unen shtub is haiz
Unde rebbe learnent kleine kinderlach
Dem aleph bais
Unde rebbe learnent kleine kinderlach
Dem aleph bais."

*see page 43 for footnotes

33

And her gentle voice rose higher and higher as the brothers and sisters sang into the night, rocking me into dreams of shtetls and foreign tongues and ages of memories I was just beginning to gather.

The raucousness of this piece was a good contrast with the quiet opening. It included the main character but placed her as an observer, someone being acted upon. She was a sponge soaking up an ordered but noisy world full of contradictions and uncertain explosions. But this was a familiar world that gave her a safe corner to grow up in.

Next, I needed to demonstrate the loss of this familiar world. In this way, the stories themselves were building conflict as well as the elements within the stories. In "Chicken Noodle Nightflights" the little girl struggles mightily to find a place that is familiar in the larger world. Just who is she when she is not in the bosom of family, as crazy as it might be.

"I remember being a little girl at the top of the stairs in somebody else's house on Grandmont Street in Detroit. A dark haired, pajama-ed visitor sitting perched and listening/glistening for some kind of sound that would soothe her and make her feel familiar in this alien atmosphere. This was Laurel's house. I often played and sometimes slept over here because Laurel was my very best friend.
We would do wonderful things together. She the blondie, SPAM eating, Singer sewing machine addict of age 7 and the pudged prisoner of chicken soup and egg challah.

Laurel could do everything that the Louisa Mae Alcott heroines could do.[13] She made all her own clothes, she played the piano like Beth in LITTLE WOMEN, she sang in her church choir. I remember going with her one Sunday, to Sunday school, and writing Hebrew words on the blackboard for her class. Laurel would make Christmas cookies, even in the heat of July—Santa Claus' or green Christmas trees. And we would eat them while drinking pink lemonade in her perfect kitchen smiled on by her Donna Reed like mother, her cat named Spook, her dog named Mitzi, her bird named HI FI and her garden with perfect marigolds. Laurel was my romantic dream child. She was everything I wasn't and I adored her for it.

*see page 43 for footnotes

It was never quite right seeing Laurel eat bagels or overstuffed tuna sandwiches. Somehow she was made for one slice of pre-sliced ham on thin white bread with French's mustard and a glass of moustache making milk. I hated milk, ham, white bread and mustard and though I adored Laurel I could never feel comfortable with the food in their house. Popcorn floating in milk. Peanut butter and banana sandwiches. I would always carefully explain to her mother, Mrs. Montague, that the reason I couldn't eat white bread and milk was because white bread and milk were not kosher—and neither was Cheerios's or bananas or eggs with loose yolks—or any other food that I couldn't stomach at the moment. Being Jewish had its great advantages. Mrs. Montague would just smile in her rapturously thrilling Donna Reed way and let me do as I please.[14]

I remember the sleep over times the most though. We would always sleep in her Sister Barbara's room. It had a soft affluent roar of an air conditioner and I would always feel properly tucked in but somehow sterilized in the matching twin beds with their matching dust ruffles and the big picture of Jesus hanging over me from the wall.[15]

Hi Jesus. Are you sleepy? I'm not. You sure are glowing. I learned a song about you the other day. It goes: JESUS LOVES THE LITTLE CHILDREN. ALL THE CHILDREN IN THE WORLD. RED OR YELLOW BLACK OR WHITE. CHILDREN SINGING IN THE NIGHT. JESUS LOVES THE LITTLE CHILDREN OF THE WORLD.

Phew. It's hard or me to sleep here. I miss my mom. She sings to me just like I sing to you. She sings: "In dem beit ha mikdash, in a vinkele cheder, zizt de al one bat zion alayne. Raisins, almonds and honey. Shluf my kinderlach, shluf."[16]

That's Yiddish. You know that language? No. Guess not. You know, Jesus. It sure is quiet here. Everybody is asleep. Bet they're not at my house. My Mom and Dad always stay up late watching Jack Paar. Bet they're up right now. Bet they're having tea and black bread and butter. It tastes real good. Not at all like Wonder Bread. Maybe somebody is up downstairs. I gotta go see. Bye Jesus.

*see page 43 for footnotes

Nope. Nobody here. So QUIEEEEETTTTTTT! The carpet sure is scratchy. DING DONG DING DONG. DING DONG DING DONG! DONG! One o'clock. I can just barely see the top of the grandfather clock. Glad the piano light is on because it's so dark here, and I think I better. I mean I really oughta. I mean I just have to go home! MRS. MONTAGUE! I WANNA GO HOME![17]

Mrs. Montague would come graciously, bathrobedly forward. Ask me what my pain was. Try to convince me that the crisp cool sheets were inviting and finally induce me to swallow down an aspirin buried in a mound of strawberry jam. But that did not work. The strawberry jam here only reminded me of the spoon of jam that my Grandfather put into his glass of tea and I was sure that here in Laurel's house, tea and jam had never even been dreamt of together. I had to go home.

So, phone calls and late night whispers agreed that that was best and my Father in a 1 AM face drove up his Buick to the WASP mansion of my very best friend, and wrapped me up and took me home."

From this childhood rescue, I brought the girl forward through several other experiences. She becomes the object of desire for a closeted gay woman, falls in love with the big shot at the synagogue but finds she does not measure up. She loses her father, leaves home, and travels to Berlin where she recognizes herself in the eyes of a young girl in a photo who is being loaded onto a truck for a trip to Auschwitz. She is betrayed by the community that spawned her with a rape attempt in the Orthodox section of Brooklyn and then, comes home as a young adult to confront the madness of her mother. The story comes full circle, with an attempt to create safety and security from the same roots as her mother did. She is too young at the end of the play to know if this will work or not.

QUESTIONS TO PONDER:
What question are you asking the audience with each story you are choosing?
Is each story asking: What do I do now? What am I learning? How will I survive? Can you help me understand?
Each story must ask the audience an active question that they can chew on.

*see page 43 for footnotes

## WHO WILL LISTEN?

In this case, I simply told this story. I did not attempt to hit a particular audience. It was later that I learned that marketing and audience development should always be considered when embarking on the solo path. But without my planning it, this play hit a chord with the Jewish community. Though the Ensemble Studio Theatre in New York, a mainstream theatre company produced it, the Jewish community took it up as sign of life in the post- World War 2, post Holocaust generation.

Here was a contemporary Jewish journey that acknowledged the Nazi period but was not Holocaust literature. The work represented a rebirth in the community thirty years after the War. This meant that the Jews had survived and were moving, intact, toward a future with a new generation. The National Foundation of Jewish Culture embraced the play and playwright, asking me to help create an initiative across the country to develop other such pieces.

This was a residual effect of the work. I did not start out to write for or about the Jewish community nor does any of my work aim for such parochialism. What this work revealed to me was that my truth was most clearly expressed in terms of the middle class American Jewish experience. But it spoke both to Jews and non-Jews alike.

I learned that the more you are who you are as an artist, the better your work becomes. Pretending you are someone else removes you from the passionate core of your selfhood. Even if you come from a place that you'd rather no one know about; realize that this place is the place that gives you life and fire. Make friends with it, roll around in it, but avoid it at your peril. Consider how your personal stories reflect and define the world from which you emerge. Observe yourself but observe yourself in the world you are coming from, especially if you are uncomfortable with the definition that this world tends to give you. Here is the conflict of your piece.

### QUESTIONS TO PONDER
How does the world you come from inform your work?
Are you a product of a particular culture?
Does that frame your experience in anyway?
Who is your audience? Who, specifically, are you talking to?
Why?

A SERIES OF SHORT STORIES
This piece was written with short stories. This allowed the actress and the audience to have a little break between each scene where both could regroup, digest and move ahead. This is only one structural possibility. Later I will discuss more fully the monologue as play and the differences between that kind of play and this. It has to do with sustaining a mood. In the long monologue/play usually the actor plays one character and we watch the character move through one experience. There is a different kind of modulation to that kind of performance. Here, each story represents another age and aspect of the main character and the breaks in action and story line help us to make those leaps without having to do Marcel Marceau pantomime to move through the ages of Man.

REFLECTIONS OF A CHINA DOLL opened at the Ensemble Studio Theatre in November of 1977. Directed by Barbara Tarbuck, designed by Christopher Nowak, it toured the United States, Canada, England and France for five years. This play spoke simply from a young woman's experience, allowing the audience to join the Storyteller in confronting the obstacles presented to her. With each challenge, the audience was able to further enter the experience of the Storyteller. They were able to root for the Storyteller and her eventual success.

This play used autobiography and the Storyteller/Performer as the main character. The storyteller was the "I" of the piece and "I" addressed the audience directly, personifying other characters from her point of view. Characters within the stories were delineated in performance by focus changes and slight vocal and physical adjustments. They were all created from "I's" point of view. It was always clear that the characters were observed and shared by the Storyteller with the Audience. You can use both first and third person in the same piece but be aware of the shift of point of view and what that does to you as performer and writer. As performer, third person takes you out of the moment and lets you observe the story. First person keeps you right in the center, allowing you to use narrative as action.

QUESTIONS TO PONDER
Do your stories emerge as first person accounts? (i.e. I did this and then I did that) Or third person accounts: ("She did this, she did that.") Observe the difference in power between these two voices.
Decide which effect you want?

> Do you want to observe yourself with the audience or do you
> want to just tell them something.

In this play, the language and narrative told the story as much as
dialogue or monologue might normally do. The description of the
synagogue or Laurel's house was as personal as what was said in
each location. So, "I" as the actress/playwright made points with the
language that I chose. In describing the girl on the steps of Laurel's
house I chose to describe myself as "listening/glistening" rather than
say I "listened and glistened." Mrs. Montague came graciously and
"bathrobedly forward". The child was "pajama-ed". The father had
on his "all day white shirt". All these word choices help us to observe
the child, seeing what choices are important to her. At the same time,
we enter her experience. Be aware of the language that you choose
and allow it to become a character in the piece as well.

## AND THE WORLD LOOKS LIKE?

And finally, make a decision about how this world is defined
theatrically. As a practical matter, keep it simple in terms of stage
wizardry. Three chairs and a bench, maximum. These props will most
likely be available wherever you go eliminating the need for a truck
or a helper to drag your set around. Most solo plays are designed to
tour and that means they can and should be able to happen anywhere
from a huge stage to the back of a John Deere tractor. No kidding. I
actually did parts of this play from the back of a John Deere tractor in
Iowa one very chilly winter.

Also, be aware that if you embark on the solo path, you are not always
going to be welcomed to a beautifully outfitted theatre with lights
and sound and seating. More likely you will be in someone's living
room, or the far end of a gymnasium while a basketball game is going
on at the other end, or at a podium with a mike that shrieks every time
you open your mouth. I have been blessed with all of these venues. It
has been challenging.

## CREATING YOUR SPACE

This next section may appear entirely too "touchy-feely" for the non-
performer but I offer the perspective anyway because I have found
that it is essential to a successful presentation. When you are touring
from space to space, you must find a way to somehow quickly make
that space your own. Just like a car in winter needs to be warmed up,
so a performance space needs to be energized in order to work and
support your performance energy.

When touring, I always ask for at least an hour in the space with no one else there. That means, the kids chess club has to find an alternative space to practice and the ladies auxiliary has to clean up before you get there. If they tell you they have to pay the janitor for an extra hour, tell them its part of the contract. You might even put this provision in any letter of agreement that you have.

Cookies and coffee are to be made in the first act in the kitchen but they have to be put together quietly. Get people used to the idea that you are a real person. Not a movie image and that everyone must join forces to create a space that will support the play. They are part of making the space ready. Ideally, you want everyone speaking quietly and begging your pardon for interrupting although it's their church and you've just shown up fifteen minutes before. In the time of Greek drama this would be called, making the space sacred. What with all the nut cakes and cults running around the country, it might be better just to ask for privacy, but for you as the performer, carry the knowledge that what you are indeed doing is making the space sacred.

All that means is that after you set your props and see if the sound system works, you take a moment to walk through the house row by row. Sometimes I do this while going over lines, more often I do this while doing vocal warm-ups, singing songs that get me off the freeway and here in the space that is mine for the evening.

The sound of my voice and my physical presence must be in every corner of the room that I will be transforming. It's not a very big deal. It's a simple gesture of taking over the space, becoming part of its energy. Practically speaking, you can also observe sightlines from the audience, hear the dead spots in the house, change seating arrangements if the chairs are too far from the stage, or in row after row of unstaggered straight lines. The only people who will see you in this kind of an arrangement are the folks in the front row. If you realize that all that can be heard in the house is an echo, find some tall plants in the hallways and drag them in to absorb sound, find partitions or curtains and gather them round to make the space less cavernous.

Take the initiative. Rearrange chairs with your stage manager, or if you have no one with you, by yourself. Sometimes, in a huge cafetorium with no incline for seats, you are better off doing the piece on the floor in front of the stage and rearranging the chairs around you in three sections making a circle. Or perhaps you want to arrange a circle of chairs around you on the stage if it is huge. You want to be able to make contact with the audience and if they are three miles away, that may be tough.

Everyone will be unhappy with such boldness. They think your job is just to say the words. But know better. The space must support you or the creaking chairs and bad sightlines will defeat you before you begin. Forego lights before you forego sightlines. If they cannot see you, they will not be able to hear you either. It's a strange rule of the theatre. Know the basics and make it your business to get them right.

Be prepared for curtain speeches. Especially if you are being booked into a campus or a community group, there will always be someone exhorting the gathered to contribute to the tag sale next week, or not forget the Tuesday meeting. These curtain Speakers usually enjoy their moment in the sun and you must be prepared for the fact that they will totally shatter any kind of pre show illusion you may have tried to create. So, always have a boom box available. Bring it with you and plug it in wherever you can. Onstage in plain sight is just fine. Have at least one full CD—forty-five minutes—of preshow music available to you. Stop the music when the Speaker arrives. Then, when the Speaker finishes, start a preshow cue of at least 30-45 seconds so the audience will return to your world on your terms. You may have to turn on the music yourself so be prepared to make it part of the first beat of the show. Then, gather your resources, your sense of humor and your concentration and begin to spin out the world that you have brought with you. Let it float out from you like a silver cord that will wrap up those in your audience and bring them along on your journey. This is especially important in a play such as the one we have been discussing. This play depends on a build of energy from beginning to end. It is a whole and each piece must find its balancing position so that the whole will work. You have a bit more flexibility in the cut and paste presentations we will discuss next, but here, you must be in charge of how the build will occur.

In the third act of VANITIES, I had a speech in which I flung my left arm out over the audience. After I had done that speech a few hundred times, I could literally see the silver cord of my energy floating out over the audience. I could see the strength of my concentration and realized that I created that pulse. So, you find the pulse of life within your performance, cast it out over those who are there to share your experience and gather them close for the ride.

These kinds of plays, especially now at the dawn of the 21$^{st}$ century, are tough to pull off. There are many people, too many perhaps, who are interested in telling us their personal stories. Many of these folk fail to connect these stories with something larger than themselves. Be tough on yourself because your competition will be. Make sure your stories are important enough to you to put them out in the world instead of giving them lovingly to your family archive.

QUESTIONS TO PONDER
Why should someone listen to these stories, stay seated during your play?
What do you want from the audience? They are your other character so how will you engage them?
Are you speaking in your most passionate, most active, voice?

If you have good answers to these questions then go ahead and be brave, and passionate. "Out of yourself, create."

---

**Footnotes:**

—Page 29—
[1] Use rich images to define your space early on. Language can be helpful in cueing your audience as tone of the piece and the kind of listening you are asking of them.
[2] Notice how the image can create the idea of safety. A canopy of fringe, hidden next to her father, safe and secure. It also identifies the child as one who has her own inner life, and time to use it.
[3] This brings us out of the child's world and back into the larger space. A chance to differentiate in text and performance adding layers and complexity to the work.

—Page 30—
[4] Good chance to define the physical space with the gaze of the actor and then let the world get smaller as the child falls asleep and the actor reels the audience into her nap.
[5] Arpege was the quintessential perfume of middle class matrons in the late 50's early 60's. The sensual image further defines the world. Again, it reinforces the sensual safety the child rests in.
[6] Reassertion of the levels of the world we are building. External world wins and wakes the child. She gets up and runs to more comfort—cookies. This is a theme of the piece as a whole. Running from safety to the real world and returning to safety—only to find that it isn't always there.

—Page 31—
[7] Her world is about to get larger as she views it from her special viewing stand.

—Page 32—
[8] Establishing the existing family, each separate from the child.
[9] Chaos reigns! Individual personalities begin to emerge.
[10] But the noise does not enter her own world of safety until the whole family gets into the act.

—Page 33—
[11] And even in the chaos there is familiarity and a place to be herself on her own terms. Just watch and listen.
[12] Here is the first time the narrator's voice directly addresses the audience. The main character of the child has been set in a strong enough position to leave her as memory object and establish the voice of the current Storyteller, an adult with another perspective on the world. Again, another layer of complexity.

—Page 34—
[13] The great admiration of the OTHER. Recognition that there is much good about the EXTERNAL world. The question is, can she find a niche where she can exist?

—Page 35—
[14] Donna Reed is NOT Jewish! Meaning, as lovely as Laurel's mother is, she is still much too lovely to be loving.
[15] For this child, Jesus is the ultimate alien! But even here, in her terror, she tries to make friends and finds some comfort.
[16] Trying to recreate her own sense of home for someone else—Jesus will do.

—Page 36—
[17] She doesn't make it, but ultimately learns a lesson about trusting the larger world.

## ELEMENTS OF THIS SOLO PLAY

### AUTOBIOGRAPHICAL ARC
This piece used the life of the performer for its arc. Each short story moved the storyteller and the audience through a character arc that asked the questions over and over again: "Where do I go now? What is so important about this lesson? How does it lead me through the story?"

### SHORT STORY FORM
In choosing the short story form, I was able to use narrative as action. I could step away from the "girl" in the story and observe her along with the audience. Note in the next section on ADAPTATION how narrative and language can become active in performance.

### DIRECT ADDRESS TO THE AUDIENCE USING AUDIENCE AS SECOND CHARACTER
In performance, I used the audience as my listener. I did not ignore the audience. I spoke directly to them. In other types of solo performing, the performer pretends the audience is not there, but here the audience was essential to the dramatic action. If they didn't receive the story, there was no interaction, no permission to move forward. This is an acting concern rather than a writing concern. The actress makes friends with the listeners, getting them on her side and asking them to figure out this life with her.

### ONE STORYTELLER
There is one storyteller in this piece. Everything comes from one speaker and every other character that is presented, is presented through the eyes and point of view of the Storyteller.

## NOTES:

Susan Merson as Mort in FAMILY SECRETS
Credit: Detroit Jewish News

## II. "INQUIRIES"- THE PRACTICAL TEACHING TOOL:
### Finding Your Pragmatic Voice

CHINA DOLL caused a great stir in my career. For the first time, I realized that I had some control over my working life. I could generate work and locate an audience. I thought I had really made strides when the New York theatrical trade papers advertised for a "SUSAN MERSON type" shortly after the great success of VANITIES. Alas, this guaranteed no work. When my agent inquired after this particular job for me, she was told that they wanted a "SUSAN MERSON type" but not necessarily SUSAN MERSON. True. Hard to believe but very true. I figured out quickly that one success and a solo piece did not make an entire career. So, I kept performing and making contact with audiences across the country and even around the world.

This was exciting but there was a side to this independence that worried me. Since CHINA DOLL was so "Jewish", it was a natural for the Jewish community. That was okay but I began to be worried that I would be pigeonholed and unable to have my work as an actress accepted across the board commercially.

I have since learned that perhaps having a niche and a definition as an actress may not be so bad. At least when the casting people do think of a particular type, you will be on their list. I spent many years trying to demonstrate my versatility however all it did was confuse the casting people. How could the same actress be adept at comedy and drama, sing and write? It didn't fit. Lessons learned late are still valuable. There is much of me that loves the expansion into new areas as an artist. Perhaps you feel the same way. But this expansion may be more interesting to you than your agent or the people he works with to get you employed.

But, the question remains—how do you keep yourself viable as a commercial "product" in the market place but grow as an a actor? I

49

was concerned about this and found that the COMPILATION solo piece is excellent at meeting both those goals. Creating such a solo piece is one way to keep your chops and be paid for it. You create a piece with any theme and find the audience that it fits.

After some time of touring CHINA DOLL, it was time for me to reconnect to the broader theatre world. There was a wonderful organization working out of New York in the late 1970's and early 1980's called Affiliate Artists. This organization brought solo artists into communities across the country for extended stays as artists in residence. Hearing about the organization and making inquiries, I was very pleased when I was asked to join their roster. It was well-paid work. Extremely unusual and downright dignified, I thought. It was an offer I couldn't refuse.

My job was to develop what Affiliate Artists called an Informance. An informance was nothing more than a compilation of material on a particular theme that could be presented in formal and informal settings. Actors, dancers, singers, musicians and conductors of all stripes were a part of the organization and I remember the evening that we all performed for each other. In the room was a young Bill T. Jones improvising movement to the jazz percussion of a young man later to work with a leading jazz combo. Metropolitan Opera finalists sang their hearts out and ballerinas soon to work under George Balanchine in the corps at New York City Ballet leapt across the party room at the small restaurant across from Lincoln Center.

In my eight years working under the Affiliate Artists banner I worked as an artist in residence in North Carolina, Iowa, Illinois. Long Island and Staten Island, New York. I performed in factories, churches, living rooms, parking lots, shopping malls, country clubs, schools, television and radio affiliates, colleges and on the back of several flat bed trucks. I would be called for a week here or there and I would steel myself for my encounter with the real world. Ah, the provincialism of the artistic New Yorker. I never wanted to leave the streets of Manhatttan despite the lure of real work. Eventually I came around but at first, I hated it!

How was I to get people's attention when they were eating baloney sandwiches and I was spouting Shakespeare? What happened to my precious "sacred space" when a calliope was piping music behind my performance area? How could I make people understand that I was a real person and not a film image and that I could see and hear them as well as they could hear and see me? Challenges abound in this kind of community setting.

QUESTIONS TO PONDER:
Are you willing to be flexible in your artistic needs in order to develop such a piece?
Are your technical skills as an actor solid enough to withstand faulty sound systems, rude audiences?
Is your desire to do this kind of performing strong enough to overcome the external challenges?
Are you passionate about working as an artist in this setting? Why?

I was extremely ambivalent when I began my stint as a solo performer with this organization. I had to come to terms with my idea of the theatre. My fantasy was to be part of the theatre I had read about as a young girl. This was the theater of Katharine Cornell and Kaufman and Hart. This was a theatre that had repertory companies and large cast plays running on Broadway. This was a theatre that existed in a time when there was no television. The movies were rudimentary and hardly a threat to the cultural claim that the theatre and its artists had on the landscape. I wanted to do new work but classics as well and I wanted it to be simple and clearly accepted as a valued and compensated part of our American cultural scene. I had to get over that.

I have asked you to consider for yourself why you are thinking about working in this area. It is an important consideration. You have the opportunity to introduce people who have never seen a live performer to that special skill that you have. You can introduce them to literature they have never been exposed to. You can show them the way that they, in their everyday lives, can use their own energy to gather strength and make changes to their world. And you can probably earn a little money to sustain yourself as an artist. Not much, since the budgets in most organizations are small and few administrators understand the value of live performance. But, this is a worthy path. Are you willing to jump in?

You will learn a great deal about people and their hopes and dreams. A monologue you choose may just be the exact crystallization of a feeling with which someone in your audience is struggling. You also will hone your technical skills vocally and physically. To command such an audience takes energy and concentration. You will need both to succeed in any venue in the performing arts.

The people you will meet will teach you a great deal about survival and hope. In the middle of winter I lived in the Weyerhauser mansion on the campus of Augustana College in Moline, Illinois. The building was old and creaky and had a spirit life of its own, especially after dark. The bathtub was enormous and the towels they left for my use were like postage stamps. It was cold and lonely and the spiky Kronos quartet, a leading new age, classical jazz ensemble, was upstairs twanging radiators till midnight to make music. They, too, had been booked into this snowy campus. They moved above me but never materialized into human beings. Just blasts and twangs from strange metal origins. I was in the ultimate cocoon with too much time to think.

So, every night I wrote. I described the high ceiling-ed room and imagined its earlier inhabitants. I wrote about the people who I had met during the day. I observed every detail. The smell of the cleaning polish, the crunch of the snow, the acne of the grad students and the bibles clutched in one hand which hid copies of Playboy Magazine. The cocoa was often cold and bland and the rooms were overheated. Everything was grist for the mill. The woman who was my host in the Quad cities particularly fascinated me.

Lois Mitchell was a strange bird. Crushed by too many snowy winters she spent her waking hours in a battered convertible that she refused to part with as an act of rebellion against the nine months of wintry weather that she fought every year. To hear her tell it, she hated her husband, her children and their three dogs. But she loved the theatre. She used to tell me she really preferred visual arts because no one talked back at her, but in truth the theatre was the art form in which she found comfort.

I don't think she realized that she became a real part of the theatre via the following story. It became a staple of one of my compilation shows, character sketches about people I met on the road. I always set it up with the basic story about Affiliate Artists and the gifts that we, the performers, receive along with our pay. It's meant to be a sketch rather than a story and it bridged other material.

## LOIS MITCHELL

The woman I worked for on that February winter road assignment had dull hyena eyes. She locked me into the aging Weyerhaeuser mansion on the snowy campus every night, cautioning me not to go out. Security refused to give me a key. She closed the door firmly, gleeful at having trapped her very own Rapunzel. She jumped into her idling convertible and cackled as she drove away to her jagged tri-level on the muddy banks of the icy Mississippi.

The main sport here was mud wrestling. The main industry, a rickety college of chiropractic that mangled Midwestern backs at five bucks a crack. One bar cloned from a nationwide chain, storefront Baptist churches. Cars rusting in the brutal winter lounged on street corners along with many a disappointed and wildly self-righteous eye.

Lois kept me as her very own. I was her gift to the community and she followed my moves with anxious self-satisfaction. When I was naughty with an outspoken "hell" or "damn" her glee was paramount for she got the joy of a vicarious "fuck you" aimed at this slushy hell without having to bear any of the responsibility for uttering it.

Across the river from Lois, I slept in a tired antique bed under eaves that sighed every hour. An exclusive Lutheran college held me captive and when I was not performing in church basements, I stared out the frosty windows of my Victorian tower or took long, deep baths in the ancient tub. I thought about the kids on the campus all so blond and white and clammy. I thought of clam chowder and why I hated it. And then the wind blew, branches broke and icicles clattered to the ground.

For lunch at the "Dairy Belle", Lois ordered me Campbell's soup with a plastic spoon. I asked her for some supplies for my confinement. I pleaded lack of moral fiber, requesting a television or radio to pass the midnight hours. She gave me a deprecating smile.

"I never watch it myself. It takes me off my game. But I'll cater to your weakness. I've one or two myself, they tell me."

Her wan smile traveled to the dreary eyes reflected back at her in the mirror above and behind my head.

"I've been hospitalized once. In Chicago. A grand town. I seem to have gone crazy here. Something about the sun. I seem to have gone crazy. Twice once. Now I do this. I employ you. Though I'm really much more interested in the visual arts." She stared at me, deeply regretting the fact that I looked back at her and blinked. She flung her disdain my way with her left glove. "I prefer things that don't move. Or dirty." Lois giggled at her own joke and the door of the Dairy Belle swung open with a huff.

Lois had two kids away at Ivy League colleges and a husband, Tom, at the office most of the time. She dressed nicely and regularly went into Chicago to shop, never staying 'til sundown.

"Do you have someone who comes home to dinner?" she asked me.
"Cronkite. Seven every night."
"Cronkite. Quite right."
And the scanning of her dead grey eyes over my forehead.

Just before midnight one endless day, after two shopping malls and a Rotary meeting, I was pondering the similarity of my current life to that of Miss America. I didn't get very far. Mary Tyler Moore was throwing her hat into the air on the snowy television screen in front of me. When the phone rang I ignored it. At midnight it rang twice more. At this time of night, prayer messages for the infidels flashed on the tube. I was beyond salvation, so I picked up the phone. The snow on the screen, and out the window and now on the phoneline sent a chill deep through me.
"Who's calling?"
"Accept Jesus as your savior and you will gladly be our neighbor at the Christ Arms, Lilly Dale Home" sang the television. And the receiver on the other end of the line clicked down.

There are no late night shows after midnight in the prairies and they say even the Baptist ministers sleep soundly through the hours of sin 'til sun up.

At 1:30 AM the television hissed and sizzled but the picture tube had given up trying to grab enough signals to create a clear picture. It was company. I dropped in and out of dreams. At three, the phone crackled and rattled. I shot up, the current running the fuse of my spine.

"Hello. It's Lois. You may find it strange for me to call at this hour but Tom's not home from the office yet and I was just wondering if you might know where my tennis racket is."
"It's a bit chilly to use your court."
"New York wit. Jew wit. Shit wit, nit wit!" She laughed on the other end of the line. The cubes in her scotch shivered.
"Are you alright, Lois?"
"I am absolutely fine. I have a fine home on the banks of the Mississippi and I'm sure I'll find my tennis racket before spring. You artists are so sensitive. Clairvoyant. Don't let me disturb your beauty sleep." Click.

I laid the receiver down on my pillow and covered it with a blanket but it refused to go silent.

Next morning we went to our last gig together, Lois and I. The Jimmy Dean Pork Sausage Plant.

From New York I sent her a tennis racket and a thank you note. I got it back with a preprinted note from Tom.
"LOIS MITCHELL PASSED QUIETLY IN HER SLEEP THE 15TH DAY OF MARCH. THE FAMILY ACCEPTS YOUR SYMPATHY."

And a handwritten scrawl. "Lois never played tennis. Lois never played at all."

> From DREAM ADJUSTMENTS, by
> Susan Merson, c. 1982

In this piece and the other ones like it from DREAM ADJUSTMENTS, the solo piece that emerged from my years on the road, I used every detail of my various confinements, as I came to know them. Road time is time out of time. A comforting anonymity enshrouds you and if you are vigilant against the demons of loneliness, you can let your eyes get big and your skin porous. The images will sustain you as an artist for many years to come. You don't need to leave home to become sensitive to your surroundings but if you're far from home, the receptors are more open; your center craves an anchor. A great time to lean into the images around you to find common ground.

After I would offer the sketch of poor Lois, a woman I considered a minor diva in the scale of things, I might introduce the audience to the grandest of divas, Amanda Wingfield, from Tennessee Williams' THE GLASS MENAGERIE. Lois was my way of sharing my perspective on the world and then offering a classic example of the same type of character. In this way, I compiled my piece as both a generative and interpretative artist. Flipping from my own material to classic material, I built the arc of my presentation.

But let's go back to developing the program itself. With Affiliate Artist, I was asked to develop a program that introduced myself to the audience as a working actress in the contemporary theatre. So, I had to decide what monologues would serve to introduce me, as I was at that time, to my audience.

HOW TO BUILD IT
My first line up went like this. It was tailored for a young actress and meant to introduce my interests as well as my abilities.

Luisa from THE FANTASTIKS by Harvey Schmidt and Tom Jones

I chose this piece because it not only offered a little glimpse into my own motivations as an actress…

"Please, God. Please! Don't let me be normal."

…it also offered a wonderful chance at poetry. The heroine brushed her hair until it turned a lovely shade of blue.

The piece had a youthful energy that would bring the audience in. I introduced it by apologizing for my own youthful romantic nature but explained that it was a classic stance, especially as written by Harvey Schmidt and Tom Jones.

QUESTIONS TO PONDER:
Is there a favorite character you know that you would really like to be? Why?

Define who the character is and how she is like and unlike your essential self. This definition will help you to commit to the theme of your presentation. By knowing this character well and why you choose her to introduce you, you will be prepared to lead your audience through the personal arc of your presentation.

FAMILY STORY from REFLECTIONS OF A CHINA DOLL
This story, printed in the first chapter, further introduced my family and the world from which I came. It allowed audiences to get to know me as a performer. I played several characters with different voices and physical mannerisms—and also let them know that being a generative artist was important to my definition of myself as a performer. (i.e. The first LUISA defines me in some ways, but here is my self-definition in my own words.) The second piece further amplifies the point of the first.

QUESTIONS TO PONDER:
What piece can you find that will broaden the context of your theme?
Are you introducing yourself? A town? A point of view?
How will the second piece amplify and further define the first. (i.e. if you are talking about being a small town creature, use the STAGE MANAGER's speech from OUR TOWN by Thornton Wilder to set up your own feelings about small town life)

JULIET- "Gallop Apace, You Fiery Footed Steeds"
ROMEO AND JULIET by William Shakespeare
By moving from contemporary to classic young women, I demonstrated flexibility as an actress, moving from contemporary to classical material, but continued the theme of unrequited love and eternal hope.

QUESTIONS TO PONDER:
How can you now take your essential theme and hold it up to the light and present another aspect of it?
If you are a young romantic, Juliet might work. If you are talking about another character that might be your alter ego, why not try a journal entry from that person. I often used the LETTERS OF CALAMITY JANE when my theme was that of an independent woman. Find some unusual source to

express the same universal theme you are offering but in other rhythms and with other references.
Do you know enough about your essential theme to do this?
Can you find the material?
Is this the place you start writing your own words?

MARY– from VANITIES by Jack Heifner
In VANITIES I played an over sexed cheerleader and in the first act of the play there is a funny monologue about the way the high school Mary handled her boyfriend's sexual advances:

"I just told him! Ted! You keep your pecker in your pants!"

This piece worked here because it was light and funny and let the audience relax and go for the ride with me. It also was an important part of my personal performing history.

QUESTIONS TO PONDER:
How can you make your audience laugh and enjoy the ride?
What do you find funny?
Does it relate to your overall theme?

CHARACTER PIECE
In this slot I chose to insert a character piece. I often used material from Colette's MUSIC HALL SIDELIGHTS or THE VAGABOND. Both works talk about performing and introduce wildly different kinds of characters. And Colette was a favorite writer, so it was another way to introduce myself to my audience.

QUESTIONS TO PONDER:
Again, how will this piece demonstrate your main theme and illustrate another part of the world of the character?
Does this express a cherished view of the performer?
Does it offer another side of your skill?
Does it introduce a writer who you admire?
What does that reveal about you—the real subject of this presentation?

POLITICAL PIECE
Here is the spot for the riskiest material. By now the audience is either yours or they have left. Because the abortion issue had recently been settled and written into law I chose that issue as one I wanted to make

a statement about. I managed to get hold of some of the testimony before the New York State Grand Jury that women have given in support of legalizing abortion. I adapted this material and presented it at this spot.

I have also used material about religion here or race relations. It can be tricky so make a judgment about how receptive you perceive your audience to be.

I once performed Jewish folktale material in a "white- Wasp-only" country club in North Carolina. At the tea following the performance, a lovely older woman with a tightly curled permanent came over to me and smiled like an alligator. Then she placed her hand on my arm and the smell of White Shoulders perfume engulfed me. I thought of Sarah Bernhardt's wish to end her life in a sealed room with flowers that would overwhelm her so she needn't face the trauma of parting from life. No need to fear mortality. I was receiving a compliment. "You're so NAH –HISE," she said through tight lips. "You shoor yoor Tjooeesh?"

QUESTIONS TO PONDER:
Do you have anything with which you'd like to challenge your audience? Have you considered whether or not they will be able to receive it or if it will be too challenging and cause you to lose their sympathy?
Think about whether you want to rock the boat or continue smooth sailing. "Pack Drama-mine."

CLOSER
This is your razzle-dazzle signature piece. If you are going to sing, here is the spot, if you are wanting to sum up the event or how you feel in general about the world and this experience, here is the place for the big finish.

QUESTIONS TO PONDER:
How do you want to leave the audience? Happy? Sad? Humming a tune or itching for a fight?
This is the slot where you give it your all and either run for the car or receive the roses. Have you done this?
Even if you never want to return to Minnesota in February, do they want you back?

59

This structure should last between 30-45 minutes depending on how much chat you insert during the piece and if you take questions as you go.

STRUCTURAL TRUTHS
Recognize that this arc, where you
>    1: get the audience's confidence through a strong statement of YOU,
>    2: give them your heart and where it comes from,
>    3: challenge their hearts with something you deeply care about and then
>    4: wrap them up with your strongest statement of self
>    5: and leave them crying

This can be applied to any subject matter or writer.

Anne Lamott in BIRD BY BIRD quotes Alice Walker as saying that the structure of a short story is as easy as ABDCE. That is, ACTION, BACKGROUND, DEVELOPMENT, CLIMAX, ENDING. You can use the same formula for developing a solo piece. Think of each piece as a component of your own personal short story. Dally here or there but basically stick to this path and you will be fine.

AUDIENCES
If you are pursuing this kind of a piece as an additional line of support for your work as an artist or entrepreneur, you now have the additional and important task of defining your audience. As I said earlier, you can create a show with this structure on virtually any topic. Have you decided who needs to hear from you?

Research the area in which you live. Are there particular interest groups in your area you feel would be receptive to a small live performance of 45 minutes? Women's organizations are always looking for speakers or programs. How about schools or coffeehouses? Call around and see who might be interested in such a presentation. No need to be in New York or London, any community has groups that would be open to this kind of work.

You can do classics or a particular writer and match your program to the needs of the high school literature curriculum. If they are studying the media, find material in the local newspaper that will illuminate the points you want to make about the coverage of a topic from different points of view. I once created a piece that discussed a political event and edited material from the New York Times, the National Enquirer, a foreign language newspaper and from Greek drama. The perspective of four different news outlets was an interesting lesson for a local Truth In Media course at several local high schools. Think creatively and be persistent in marketing your ideas. If the local school board is studying Poetry—get out your poetry books and find material that will be interesting to students. Use this as an opportunity to grow in all ways.

As a desperate young girl yearning to be in the theatre, my mother challenged me to read every book in the local library that I could find about the theatre. She told me if I read everything I found, I could find a place for it somewhere. She was right. That curiosity and recognition that anything and everything can be descriptive has sustained me through many an artistically dry period. There is always something to learn and you'd be surprised where it might show up in your work. As your intellect grows, your artistry will follow. Be careful to balance the two. Too much intellect will leave your work dry and boring. Too much juice will leave the piece without a reliable center. Find the middle balanced road, and from there, freedom. You will demonstrate the value of knowledge and the vitality of ideas through your work. The children are watching. It is not a bad thing to demonstrate to the world.

In offering this kind of program, realize that you are offering an up-close look at the process of transformation. Most young people today have not seen live performance up close. Mostly, kids are exposed to film and video or the occasional Broadway musical in a 2500 seat house. You have the chance to let young people understand that it is possible to control the environment in which they live through their own concentration and focus. Change right in front of them and then, show them how they too have personal power and energy. In a high tech, cyber world, you will be surprised at how powerful your performance work will be for such an audience.

BASIC MARKETING
Create a simple flyer that has all your performance information available:
> 1: The names and subjects of the presentations you are prepared to give or create.
> 2: The length of the show.
> 3: The target audience.
> 4: Your fee.

5: A few quotes about your work or attach a letter or two of recommendations from someone who knows your work and can recommend it.

6: Phone number or email contact information

Have an information sheet, a packet of reviews, technical requirements for the presentation. A video of your work might also be helpful but make sure it is professional. No homemade hand held tapes. You want someone to pay you real money for your services so make sure your promotional material is clear, smart looking and professional.

Give these packets to people you think are potential bookers. Follow up with phone calls and emails. Make sure you identify the person who makes the decisions and that this person receives your material. Target this list of people carefully. Material costs money to produce and you want to make sure that whoever receives it is interested enough to look at it before they throw it away. Keep a list of your contacts and make the calls to them until you get an answer one way or the other. If they say no, keep them on the list anyway. You can use it for the marketing of your next show.

Develop a list from people that you know first and ask them to recommend people or organizations that they know and where you can use their name to talk to a potential booker. Go at this systematically. You are building a business. Take this part of the job seriously.

Once you have developed a local list, hook up with national organizations that might help. There are umbrella-booking organizations for college campuses and for clubs nationally. Do your research at the library and the Internet and make sure you make the right connections.

You might even consider a website but remember that websites only work if people actually visit them. That means that the addresses must be easily accessible by the big search engines and hopefully be linked with other performing organization sites.

DO YOUR RESEARCH
Once you have identified a few target audiences who might be interested in allowing you to visit with a 45-minute presentation, spend time at local bookstores and foreign journal stands. Read whatever you can find and be on the lookout for material that will reflect your

passion. Listen to commercials, read ads, read columnists. Be a part of the world and keep your ears open for conversations that match your themes. Write them down and see if you can fashion them into monologues or a commentary on your basic themes.

Go to websites that may seem a bit odd at first glance and see if you can find statements that, when performed and placed in a context of your creating, will illuminate another group's perspective.

Make friends with your local librarian. Go to the actual library and meet the actual person rather than relying solely on the Internet for your research. Two heads are better than one and an ally at the research desk of your local branch can net wonderfully interesting perspectives and material. Also, your local librarian may know of venues that would welcome your presentation. Making friends when marketing such a program should be encouraged. You will never know who may be able to book you and enjoy your perspective on the world.

Also, get to know the "stacks" of the largest library in your area. Most primary source material these days is on microfiche but make the effort to search it out and encourage your librarian friend to give you access to open stacks where they exist. There is a wealth of dramatic material available in the everyday archival files of most libraries. This type of primary source material may inspire you to unearth documents that haven't been seen or heard from in many years. You will find the excitement of finding a real story that needs to be told.

While living in New York, I became fascinated with the early years of the great Eastern European migration. By searching the stacks at the 42nd Street library, an entire world opened before me. In THE EXILE OF SARAH K., a piece I wrote about the white slave trade at the turn of the last century, I used a great deal of primary source material about family planning, dating etiquette, poetry and popular song lyrics. I also found wonderfully evocative religious tracts that spoke of the evil of drink and the dangers of "panderers". What emerged was a portrait of a particular time and its mores. Because I was able to pick and choose material, I was able to both satirize sexual mores of an earlier time and also compare courting rituals of 14 year olds in 1903 and 1993.

A word here about using material that is still under copyright. Be aware that there are certain rules that apply to the use of published material in public performance. Double check that the material you

63

are using is in the public domain. If it is not, then call or write the publisher to obtain permission to use the material in question.

Usually, in these kinds of situations, where you are excerpting sections and most of your work is in an educational or communal setting, rights are not difficult to obtain. It just may take a little time. Do not ignore this step, however. Besides the obvious respect for the writer and her work, it can be embarrassing and complicating when you arrive to perform a few poems from a local poet and the local poet's cousin is sitting in the front row, eager to report your infraction of copyright rules. This becomes more of an issue when you do major stage adaptations of one author's work but the rules still apply here.

It's easier to obtain rights if you write the material itself.

VENUES
Many small theatre companies have difficulty raising the money needed for a public performance space. More and more companies are offering salon programs where they invite a small audience into a private home to enjoy a one on one theatre experience. These "salon" settings are perfect for this kind of solo work.

Think of community centers, libraries, festivals, and city after school programs, rehab centers, day care centers. Anywhere where people gather. I even know of one enterprising artist who gathered three fellow performers and organized a lunchtime poetry and prose performance in the food court of a shopping mall and another group that performs against the background of a pocket park in Manhattan.

AND OUT OF YOURSELF CREATE
Especially if your computer skills are lacking. Part of your responsibility as an artist is to follow the tradition of Mrs. Fiske and David Belasco and be an artist manager. Haven't heard of them? Great! Look them up. They are both wonderful subjects for solo pieces.

Create your work and create your audience.

SOMETIMES LESS IS MORE
Depending on where you are performing and in what venue, you may choose pieces that can be performed more easily from a podium in a Readers Theatre style. Often ladies' clubs etc have no place to move around and you are better off using a podium or a music stand. If is perfectly acceptable to hold script in hand in these kinds of venues. In

fact, it helps the audience to relax with the experience and match their expectations to the performance that they will see. Hand held scripts cue the audience that this is an intimate reading situation and that they are part of the process.

As a performer, you must still know the material intimately and in some ways more forcefully than if you were moving around. You must make the material come alive from behind a podium. Make sure you know it well enough to walk in front of the podium, up and down the aisles if necessary. Make sure the material is under your control even if you have a script in hand. You are still controlling the energy in the room and commanding attention and relaxing your audience.

Go and see what you can find out and then bring it on. Go ahead. We need your perspective.

## ELEMENTS OF THIS PIECE

### INTRODUCTION
Introduce your main theme and character. Set up an energetic rhythm that will capture attention.

### EXPAND THE CONTEXT
In this piece, you expand upon the theme of the first piece. Perhaps you go deeper into the background of your opening character or give the presentation a broader context from which to draw.

### CHANGE STYLE WHILE EXPANDING THEME
Here is where you do a piece with a classical style or another view of the world and main character.

### COMIC RELIEF
Again, you are continuing to define your main theme and character but let the audience laugh a little. Relax and enjoy.

### CHARACTER SLOT
Here you can try a character piece where your essential nature is disguised in another type of character. The character would have something to do with your main theme, but it is also a way to show your versatility as a performer.

### CHALLENGE PIECE
Here is the place to let a controversial piece emerge if you have one that is important to you. More closely held values revealed.

### CLOSER
Razzle dazzle closer. Loud or soft, this one sums up everything you want to show and have them feel.

**NOTES:**

Susan Merson as Grama in FAMILY SECRETS
Credit: Detroit Jewish News

## III. "THE LOVES OF SHIRLEY ABRAMOWITZ"- THE ADAPTED WORK: Losing Yourself in Someone Else's World

So, now you have two choices. You can get naked and reveal your whole life story before the world or you can pick and choose material fluidly and forever, never needing to settle into one point of view or another. Great, right? Variety is the spice of life but frankly, it can cause indigestion. I wanted just some regular "meat and potatoes" for a while. I needed to rest in my work and these pieces took a great deal to maintain.

After performing so publicly in both VANITIES and CHINA DOLL, and then touring the hinterlands with CHINA DOLL and INQUIRIES, I felt very raw. Nowhere to run and nowhere to hide when doing these two forms. One of the joys of acting for me had been the ability to melt right into the material with which I was working. But if the material itself is ME than it makes hiding a little tougher.

I was "eyeburnt" from VANITIES and dealt with that by standing tall and claiming my own space, and then I became pragmatic and fast on my feet, able to assemble and perform a play whenever—and wherever—someone was willing to listen. I had proven that I could command an audience with both my life stories and with my technical skill and intellectual interests.

HIDING IN PLAIN SIGHT
Now, I just wanted to act again. I know it may seem strange that performing on the stage can be viewed as a private act, but when you sink into character and have a strong personal center, knowing that you will not melt into oblivion, acting can be extremely relaxing and energizing. Like a meditation of sound and movement, the support comes from the world created solidly by craft and technique. Your ego is released when you act. It's not about you, it's about the character. Not having to be "on" as you all the time is so refreshing.

This time I wanted to act with friends. But I wasn't quite sure how to define those friends. And I wasn't sure if I wanted those friends as actual actors on stage with me. Yes. Wildly weird and foolish but still a motivating force.

The VANITIES experience was very difficult for me. Great friendships were betrayed, blows were dealt and I left the stage of the small theatre on West 43rd Street reeling. Truthfully, I still didn't feel I could trust other actors enough to create with them. This can be difficult when you are engaged in a collaborative art form, to say the least.

I had admired the director of VANITIES enormously. Garland Wright, who later went on to run the Guthrie Theatre Company in Minneapolis had opened my eyes to the beauty of the theatre—and beauty in general. Before we created that piece, Garland headed up the Lion Theatre Company on 42nd Street. A group of us came to New York in 1971 from a summer at the American Shakespeare Festival in Stratford, Connecticut where we, like many young artists before and since, committed ourselves to the development of a new theatre company. Garland Wright and Gene Nye founded the Lion Theatre in the living room floor of the cottage I was sharing with actresses Dianne Weist and Mary Catherine Wright on the Stratford Beach. In its first few years, the Lion created wonderfully innovative theatre.

Our first season we produced KITTY HAWK by Len Jenkin, Shakespeare's THE TEMPEST and PULP, a compilation piece for five actors modeled on Orson Welles' Living Newspaper. From one success to the next, the Lion had a few good years. Garland won an Obie for his production of "K" which was based on the work of Franz Kafka and we all immersed ourselves in the words and world of Colette's MUSIC HALL SIDELIGHTS to create a stunning visual homage to the demi-monde and European vaudeville. Draped in Garland's vision and Colette's words, we each became members of an eclectic French Music Hall troupe.

The months before we began rehearsal I saved my money and ventured to France on my own. Living in a quiet little village near the Pont du Gard in Avignon, I wanted to exorcise all the VANITIES demons and come to terms with what it meant to be on my own. Yes, I was getting over a broken heart too, but that's another story. I had already started solo performing and realized that I could be a support for myself as an artist. I guess I wanted to see how it really felt to spend a life all alone. Not good. Not necessary. Overly dramatic—but what can I say? Maybe Mom was right when she called upon the spirit of Sarah Bernhardt to protect her sensitive flower child.

I found myself sitting in French cafes for hours hoping someone would speak to me. Café owners would throw me out at closing forcing me to return to the small castle I had rented alone. I would trudge home and huddle next to the bedroom wall straining to hear the old widow next door singing French patriotic songs in her sleep. In the mornings, I communed with the little boy across the courtyard as he pee-ed out his window aiming for my coffee cup. Young couples were married and paraded through the streets. Everyone in town was invited to the weddings. The café was closed all the time for private parties. Terrible-r and terrible-r.

I got in the car and found the small village of St. Sauveur-en- Puysaye, the birthplace of Colette. With my copy of Sido's Garden, I walked the streets of her beginnings and pondered mine. She became my traveling companion and best friend, dispensing wisdom about life and love, always feeding my soul with humor and beauty. Colette took care of me those two months abroad and now I had come back to the States to bring her characters to life.

WHO SPEAKS YOUR HEART?
This relationship with Colette proved central in my growth as a solo performer. I suppose I fell in love with her. My crush led me to study and internalize much of her work. She is a great friend to have had then and to enjoy even now. I subsequently fell for Willa Cather, visiting her birthplace in Red Cloud, Minnesota. And being fortunate enough to spend a summer working in Peterborough New Hampshire, I weekly visited Willa's grave in nearby Jaffrey on my buzzy little blue motorbike. Willa, Mount Monadnock and the blue summer skies of New England got me through yet another broken heart and provided wonderful reading on the road.

I had discovered I had great friends in great writers who embraced me without judgment. Their language opened my world and I wanted to give back as much of them as I could.

Rather than going to therapy, where I probably belonged, I decided I would continue my solo path by immersing myself in the language and life of yet another writer who was speaking to me at that time. That way I could avoid having to deal with real people and still act with an entire company of characters. Some might identify this as a severe antisocial disorder. I plead no contest. I will put the motivation down to a particular time, place, love life and age.

I was back home; ready to work and I needed someone I could count on.

I had recently discovered the work of Grace Paley. Now this was a real person. A fierce, funny, brilliant survivor. She raised two kids on her own when it wasn't easy or popular to do such things, she wrote from her own life experience (which was culturally similar to mine), she lived in the Village at that time and her work had only rarely been adapted for the stage. I bought every book, essay or poem she ever wrote and swallowed her whole. She had a toughness that I recognized and a heart that I crawled right into. Better than the plaster wall and the French patriotic widow. I could learn a thing or two about life by working on her stuff.

QUESTIONS TO PONDER:
Which writers do you know that move you enough to want to give them a public voice?
What in their stories or their language speak theatrically to you?
What about their voice speaks personally to where you are at this time in your life?

As I began to look through her work, especially her short stories, I recognized how she used language rhythmically in ways that I responded to. Not only the stories appealed but also the language that would come out of my mouth. It was language and rhythm I had heard all my life. In THE LOUDEST VOICE, Paley creates a main character who opens her mouth and makes pickle brine bubble. So familiar to me! I came from a family that only spoke at hurricane volume and who seemed to have not a clue of the world around them. They too, like the heroine of this marvelous story, found a place in the world. And the descendants of these loud mouthed Jewish citizens have become actors, cantors, public speakers, lawyers and even a speech pathologist. Paley's people spoke loud and strong, with lot's of consonants and nary a self conscious breath.

Their language had its own identity. There is no way that Paley's heart would get lost in my interpretation. She is present in her prose and so the prose will easily serve as a base line to rest on and as I began working on the stage version of her work. I was thrilled.

My colleague and friend Edward M. Cohen was the literary manager of the Jewish Repertory Theatre on 14th Street at that time. He was enough of a friend that I felt I could trust him but we had never worked together. We had a clean slate. I liked his view of the world and the down to earth approach he brought to his productions. It was clean and connected. That's what I was after with this piece.

I showed the material to Ed and he too found it highly theatrical. We set to work choosing the stories that we felt would work in our project. GOODBYE AND GOOD LUCK, a hilarious story about a young woman's long time romance with a star of the Yiddish theatre, was already a contender. It had vivid characters, was about the theatre, gave an opportunity for fun—but it had its problems as a performance piece because it was written as a memory. The problem with playing a memory is that the "event' is the person remembering rather than being in the moment. The piece was passive rather than active. Remember that exercise in chapter one? Find the action, the actable line? No matter. I still felt the Paley material could work. I wanted to proceed. I needed to get the rights to the material.

WANTED DEAD OR ALIVE
When you choose material to adapt, think about whether the writer is living or dead. Macabre perhaps, but a living writer will have living thoughts and concerns and perhaps objections to the adaptation of the material they are allowing you to work on. This is eventually what happened to the Paley project. But, I was excited to develop a relationship with this writer, if not in person, then at least on the stage. A writer who is no longer with us may not be as tough to deal with. I mean by this that the estate that controls the work may be happy to have the work revived. This can cut both ways, of course.

Two writer friends have done adapted pieces and have run into some problems. Stephen Sachs, playwright and Artistic Director of the Fountain Theatre in Los Angeles wrote a wonderful adaptation of Thornton Wilder's OUR TOWN that examined the AIDS crisis in a contemporary small town. He called his version OUR TIMES. Stephen tells the story that he:

> "... just wrote it for fun. And it was wonderful but when I asked permission the Wilder estate was not interested. I didn't have the rights up front—not a good idea."

Writer Jane Anderson ran into a similar problem with her play about the painter, Matisse, which was produced as part of the Humana Festival in Louisville in the late 1980's.

> "The Matisse estate objected to the piece because some of the scenes dealt with Matisse as a very sensual and sexual artist who was trapped in the body of a bourgeois. There was one scene in particular that offended La Famille Matisse. It was really a very sweet little scenelet in which Matisse's 8-year-old son Pierre comes into his father's studio while he's painting a nude. The naked model and the boy have a very innocent exchange while Pierre sweats it out, worrying that he's corrupting his son."

Apparently, Matisse's grandson—whose dad was the infamous Pierre—objected strongly to this scene because it defames his daddy's memory. There's nothing more middle class than a middle class Frenchman."

It doesn't always have to turn out this way. Stephen Sachs gives us another anecdote about dealing with writers and their representatives.

> "... The opposite can happen. The example of good news is when I did Baron in the Trees. I did the adaptation (of the Italo Calvino short story) and we, the cast and I, worked on the project and developed it without ever having the rights to produce it. We worked on it (in workshop) for one year. The Calvino estate kept saying no. But we didn't give up. We kept working—out of love; we were committed, etc. Finally—after one year of us working on it together—permission finally came. We could open it to the public. We did and it was a huge success. So... sometimes ya gotta have faith."

And Stephen has successfully obtained rights for several other projects from writers living and dead. All of this is to say that you need to want to do the project enough to ask the question and don't take no for an answer. Unless you absolutely have to.

I was in love. I was passionate about Paley's view of the world and that propelled me forward. So, I gave it a shot.

QUESTIONS TO PONDER:
Are you sure the genre that you are choosing to adapt is suitable for performance?

Can you be honest with the writer of the primary source material that you may have to change things to get your desired effect?

How much of a relationship do you want with the primary source writer? How much are they willing to allow?

Are you ready to have creative suggestions that may alleviate the primary writer's concerns?

I managed to get the Paley's phone number in the Village. It was actually in the phone book. Always a good place to look. I boldly called her at home. My heart was pumping; terrified she would blow me off. But I absolutely felt compelled to try. I could hear the water running in the sink as she said, "Yeah. Go ahead. But don't change any words." I don't think she even heard my name.

And so it began.

Here's how Ed Cohen remembers it:

> "You brought the piece to me. I had never heard of her (Paley)! Then we both went down to Cooper Union to see her read and the personality and voice were so vivid that we both wanted to do it. We each suggested stories that we thought were right and originally we settled on four, including the one about the Yiddish actor (GOODBYE AND GOOD LUCK) which we both liked and felt sure it would be the jewel of the evening. You made the deal with Paley that we could not change a word."

We began to work on the material. We laughed a lot in rehearsal. We thought we were great. Laughing at our cleverness! Always dangerous. Here's how Ed tells it:

> "All through rehearsals we were sure we had a winner but the minute we put it up—even at the first run through we did for kids who worked there—it was clear it wasn't holding. At the first read through at New Dramatists for E.S.T. (Ensemble Studio Theatre), we both got depressed. It got worse at the E.S.T. run through; where it was clear people minds were wandering. And you were having trouble memorizing verbatim, which diluted the strength of the voice we had both fallen for."

77

A painful but accurate memory from my friend.

THE RIGHT PARTNER
Here is as good a place as any to discuss the right companion for a
solo journey. The right director is key. He has to be someone who will
tell you the truth and from whom you can hear it. Someone like Ed
who just tells the truth—when he has to—and that's what was perfect
for me.

The COMPILATION PIECE is one that you can probably work on
and put together alone but both the AUTOBIOGRAPHICAL and
ADAPTATION forms need another eye. The eye is on the script as
well as on you as a performer. The eye of the director creates the
construct of the piece as a whole so you can relax and worry first
about the text—with your built in dramaturg; and then go ahead, forget
the text, trust that the director will show you when it's not working,
and then focus on being an actor.

This is an intimate process and relationship. For CHINA DOLL, I
asked a wonderfully talented friend and colleague, Barbara Tarbuck,
to work with me. Barbara and I came from the same neighborhood in
Detroit. She knew the characters I was writing about and had shared
most of the events in my story. In fact, she has shared her insight as an
artist with me freely and generously most of my life. It was Barbara
who introduced me to E.S.T. and it was Barbara who introduced me
to Affiliate Artists. I trust her like family. And we are still close to this
day. Our work together on CHINA DOLL was very productive. This
director knew the material the context and me. She had my respect
and trust, and I had hers.

Not that the whole process was smooth. There were bumps. Instructive
moments forced us to define ourselves in our roles as actor/writer
and director/dramaturg/friends. We learned about the importance of
respect for each other's process and each other's personal needs. We
learned about jealousy, praise, and the danger of both. But Barbara
and I shared a common vision and she was a perfect director for my
first project.

When it came to a foray into an adapted work, I needed to find someone
with all of those qualities that Barbara possessed and more.

Trust and respect go without saying. This time, I also needed a real
strong sense of humor, an understanding of comedy, and of Jewish

and New York culture and rhythms. I was from the Midwest, after all, and New York rhythms, though familiar, were then something I needed to double check. Ed and I had met when I was doing a very bizarre little play at the Cubiculo Theatre in which I, and a number of other actors—including Kathy Bates—sat in a row and said a series of random words. I believe I said the word "debris" about 25 times in the course of a 10-minute section. I was really trying to give that word some oomph—but I just couldn't find it.

 A man across the room watched my reaction as my director, Paul Cooper, told me sincerely to come up with more "connected caring" for the word "debris". Now there was a stumper. My face registered every part of my confusion and that man, Ed Cohen, who was directing the dance version of this masterpiece, laughed out loud at my expression. I had made a friend. We subsequently were involved in the Jewish Theatre Association at the National Foundation for Jewish Culture and several other projects.

When the Paley piece came up, Ed, as Literary Manager of Jewish Rep, was bringing in and producing young writers like Donald Margulies (who eventually won the Pulitzer Prize for Drama in 2001 for DINNER WITH FRIENDS.) I was appearing in a short play at JRT by Donald about Delmore Schwartz called IN DREAMS BEGIN RESPONSIBILITY. Ed had set the project up and I liked his taste. He was a stabilizing presence during rehearsals and I liked the feel of the productions that he had mounted. He had also published a novel and knew how language functioned in both fiction and plays. And I didn't think he was any nuttier than I was. A good match.

QUESTIONS TO PONDER:
Is your director knowledgeable about the style you are working in?
Does she have dramaturgical skills?
Can she help you to get a production of the work?
Is this important to you? Are you willing to share both profits and glory with this person?
Are you willing to hear the truth from them?
Does she make you laugh?
Does she make you feel brilliant?

LETTERS OF AGREEMENT
Ed and I decided to define the terms of our relationship early on. Ed was the first director with whom I had a contract. We were clear

about what work we were to do together, who got credit for what and if the shows were to be produced by a mainstream producer, who would get what percentages of the fees.

I remember I felt that it was foolish at the time to work out all these details for a project that would net no more than 20 dollars in profit, but in the end, it made sense. It made us both aware of our commitment to the project and to each other.

You can make the Letter of Agreement very simple. No need to go to a lawyer at this point. Just put down the facts and if there are issues that are important but not relevant to the moment, agree to negotiate them later.

Just state the name of the project, the roles that each of you will play. Take it one step at a time:

> Dear Ed:
> This letter will set out the parameters of our working relationship in the development and presentation of "THE PALEY PIECE". You will be DIRECTOR and CO-ADAPTOR and I will be ACTRESS and CO-ADAPTOR

How long is the commitment to the project in force?
> This agreement will be in force through the workshop phase of the work. That means, from now through the time that a Producer comes in and agrees to invest more than 2000 dollars in the production of this work or three months, whichever comes first.

How can we get out of it?
> We agree that we can terminate our agreement under the following conditions: Artistic differences. (i.e. if we want to and/or, we hate each other and we no longer enjoy the process of working together.) Either party can initiate discussions about termination of our relationship.

Do you retain rights to the authorship?
> Because I brought the original material to you, we agree that if we terminate our relationship, I retain rights to the project for a period of one year. I will have to do my own adaptation unless I pay you to perform your adaptation. This to be negotiated in good faith at the appropriate time.

Do you get a credit in the program that says you originally developed the project?

> The program credit shall read: "ORIGINAL ADAPTATION OF THIS WORK BY EDWARD M. COHEN AND SUSAN MERSON WITH THE EXPRESS PERMISSION OF GRACE PALEY".

Do you agree to renegotiate if some real money or real opportunity arises for the project?

> At the end of the three-month period or the injection of over 2000 dollars into the process, we will determine how to proceed to the next step. We reserve the right to each take a producing credit at that time to be negotiated in good faith.

What happens if a star comes along and wants to do the work?

> Merson reserves the acting rights to this project for a period of three years. Cohen does the same for directing rights. Either party can give up their artistic position for a negotiated royalty fee and a Producing/Adapter credit, to be negotiated in good faith.

The elements of such an agreement are arbitrary. They mostly focus the work and commitment of the artists. There is very little money to be made but one wants to be clear about basics. The short term of such an agreement allows you to renegotiate and put in things that need to be addressed

If a Producing Organization appears, they usually have their own contracts. That's when you need to get someone to take a look at the agreement for you. In most cities, there are volunteer lawyer groups for the arts. You can call your local bar association to find someone who might help.

Do not make the mistake of negotiating a Broadway show at this stage of the game. This is a project that comes from love and it must be treated that way. No one is going to steal anything from anyone— right now. Add a large dose of faith into this situation and you will better off. If you think the other guy is a crook before you begin, begin with someone else.

Yes, I have had material stolen from me. Yes, I have been ripped off. I am still owed money from producers that never paid off a commitment in an Off Broadway Show. Oh well. I know that Chazz

Palmintieri and Anna Deveare Smith and John Leguizamo and Spalding Grey—among lots of other artists—have all had television projects made from their work. So what? Get the work done first and then get the lawyers involved. Sometimes you will win and sometimes you lose. At this stage of the game, get the work done in good faith and then move forward. You are only committing to a three-month period.

Good. Got that straight? Let us proceed.

HONORING THE PRIMARY WRITER'S VOICE
Now, this is the hard part. As I wrote earlier, our first version of the Paley stories was dismal. Here's Ed's memory:

> "The Yiddish actor story—that we both loved—did not work at all. It went on too long, there was too much exposition, the story line was too complicated to work and although the voice of the narrator was wonderful, everything she was saying was in the past so there was nothing to play, nothing was happening to her!"

And Ed does go on! Listen to this:

> "And it got worse! I remember you entered and mimed kicking away a kid's skateboard and some friend of yours said she thought you were a five-year-old who had fallen off it. My son said the language was so dense for the first five minutes he couldn't figure out if you were speaking English. The audience didn't know who you were or where and the stories remained stories and definitely not a play! I suggested that we forget the whole thing and you were immensely relieved."

Everything Ed said was true. It was a mess. Here I had taken my love and placed it on the stage and I had really blown it. Time to regroup and rethink. We took some time off. I tried to forget the sound of coughing, embarrassed friends avoiding my gaze as I plodded through this event. And then I came to terms with a great truth.

LANGUAGE and RHYTHM are great, but if they are on a stage, they have to BOW TO ACTION.

Let me say that again: LANGUAGE AND RHYTHM MUST BOW TO ACTION. Remember action in actable material?

There is no way around it. The main character must have an understandable journey. She has to have a compelling "need-to-know" or an objective for the overall action of the piece. She must have a vital, uncluttered relationship to either the audience or the other characters being created on the stage. So, what does that mean? With most fiction it means, CUT. You are not performing a short story; you are performing a play based on a short story so adjustments must be made, even if they are painful. I love poetry. I love images and all the depth that a novel can give us but it is not a play, so get tough and look at your material again and find your arc.

QUESTIONS TO PONDER:
Who is your main character?
How does that character emerge in the story?
Is she speaking in first person—"I did this and then that?"
Are all the people that she relates to connected in any way?
Are they easy enough to keep track of?
Can they be defined physically, vocally and with language?

These are the same questions that need answers in the AUTOBIOGRAPHICAL solo play. Except this time, you need to understand the basic need and instinct of the primary writer and try to honor that voice. That is the voice that called you to the material.

With the problems at the earlier performances, I was not eager to continue working with this material but once again, pragmatism reared its familiar head.

Ed and I were contacted by the National Foundation for Jewish Culture and asked if we would take the piece to Israel as part of the Tel Aviv Festival. This was a wonderful opportunity but I did have my reservations. Here's how Ed tells it:

"When the possibility of going to Israel arrived, I remember you bellowing to me over the phone. 'I don't want to go half way cross the world to turkey'. It was then that I figured we were going far away, we might be able to experiment with the stories and I said: (expletive deleted) it! Let's cut! So, at the first reading at your house for Israel, I gave you my cuts. Your eyes lit up with the concept and you picked up your pencil and went even further than I had. I also brought you the new story of the 'Faith' character visiting her father in the hospital which worked only because we just used the central core of the story and cut out (most of) the fancy wordage. It was then we decided to make the narrator one character rather than a series of different voices."

We dropped the Yiddish actor story and chose THE LOUDEST VOICE, which is about a little girl who is chosen to narrate the Christmas pageant at her elementary school because she has the loudest voice. Her pride at such an achievement and the fact that she is a child of Jewish immigrants and culturally the least likely choice for such a job adds to the conflict and humor of the piece. The text gave many opportunities for acting fun. I could create a wonderfully kind WASP teacher and a loud-mouthed little girl. This set up the main character of Shirley Abramowitz.

The other material that worked was in the 'Faith' series of stories that followed 'Faith' through the trials and tribulations of being a single mother, dealing with aging parents she both adored and with whom she was constantly at odds. We found our central character and built her arc—from loud-mouthed kid to struggling single mom.

Ed again:

"That's when the whole thing came together as a play instead of separate very literary stories. The rest is history—almost."

We felt confident as we prepared for the festival despite the fact that a trial run performance at a huge WASP lodge up in the Catskills was met with silent stony faces from the octogenarian Episcopals who were in attendance. It was a good exercise in concentration. I shrugged it off and prayed a lot.

We went off to Israel and, to the relief of us both, were a great success. The reviews from the Jerusalem Post were terrific and the international audiences responded to this Brooklyn woman trying to get through her colorful but difficult life with humor and fortitude. I loved this character. It was essentially the voice of Grace Paley and I thought she would be delighted with our victory.

Alas. When I spoke with her upon our return to New York her reaction was not positive. In fact, we immediately lost the rights.

First, she explained candidly, that the characters were all different, they had different names and our assumption that she would allow us to mix up her writing in that way was "way off base, kid"! Besides, it just so happened that the festival took place during the Israeli invasion of Lebanon and Ms. Paley had been picketing and protesting the invasion the entire time we were gone. Oops.

After a sound verbal political and artistic drubbing on the telephone from my hero, I quickly apologized, thanked her for letting me work on it up to that point, and went to hide in a closet.

Be careful when you fall in love that you still respect your object of infatuation. In other words, never assume that your idea of your hero's voice is the same as her idea of her voice.

Yet another reason to write your own play!

ELEMENTS OF THIS PLAY

IDENTIFY YOUR COMPELLING REASON FOR USING THIS MATERIAL.
Be clear about the passionate connection you have with the material and the writer. This passion will help you to continually focus the play. What about this writer connects with me? How does that inform the piece? Always cut the material to the arc, and to the clarity of the Main Character's "need- to- know".

DEFINE THE MAIN CHARACTER
Allow the material to shape and create a main character through action.

DEFINE THE JOURNEY OF THE CHARACTER
Make sure that the words you have are not squandered. Make the language economical so it can move the action.

CHECK THAT LANGUAGE ENHANCES RATHER THAN DETRACTS FROM THE CENTRAL ACTION
This falls into the cut and focus department.

MAKE SURE THAT YOUR VISION AND THE PRIMARY WRITERS CAN EASILY CO-EXIST
You are creating a third entity. Not your play, not the primary writer's story—but a third creature that has a life and integrity of its own that must be sanctioned by all parties.

# NOTES:

Susan Merson as Kid in FAMILY SECRETS
Credit: Detroit Jewish News

## IV: "PICNIC IN EDEN"- POETRY ON STAGE: Language As Character and Poem as Action

After the Paley piece, I scurried back to material of my own devising. I needed the freedom to work with language and have it be adaptable to the needs of the stage without insulting the writer and conceiving an idea that had nothing to do with the original intent of the material.

There were so many words to cope with in the Paley piece. Each of the words needed vitality and energy to keep an audience engaged. But the words were leisurely, not efficient. They took their time. Too much time in language and not enough time in action. Cutting it to the active arc of the piece helped it become "actable" but plays and stories are different animals.

I had met up with the work of William Carlos Williams a few years earlier and was impressed with the sparseness of his images and the way he could crystallize action. In every poem, one finds a true image that is complete. "A red wheel barrow in the rain."

A woman holding, palming and then eating the perfect plum. A flower fallen and deftly placed on its stem again. These images have always stayed with me and given me a sense of relief. They are not busy images, they are simply true. Such is the power of poetry.
It is simple but has layers of complexity that continue to draw us in.

THE POWER OF POETRY
As I write this, poetry has regained a small, smart notoriety due to the actions of an unsuspecting First Lady Laura Bush. Mrs. Bush, a literacy advocate, cancelled a White House poetry reading that was to have occurred during the build up to a war in Iraq. She cancelled the reading because she was afraid that the poets would take the opportunity to express their anti-war opinions in their work. What a wonderful boost

to the power of poetry! Can you imagine that the White House in 2003 perceived the words of a few poets as dangerous to their plans?

The frugal words of a poet can have great power. And power is political, one-way or the other. According to Poet Laureate Wyatt Prunty, politics seek to simplify ideas. Poetry seeks to make ideas complex by crystallizing ideas to a "mental concentrate" that is dense enough to need "unpacking", one resonant idea after the other.

Lawrence Ferlinghetti speaks of the need of a poem to have a broad enough "public surface" to engage a public audience. This public surface is what snags the listener, then they are drawn inward to "concentrate" and little by little they are treated to the "unpacked ideas" as they are rolled out by a poem.

Veteran actress Salome Jens created a remarkable solo piece based on the poetry of Anne Sexton called ABOUT ANNE. She has performed it internationally to well-deserved celebratory reviews. She is clear that only certain kinds of poems lend themselves to "acting" and to the creation of a play. A poetry play defined as a "series of events that create an arc—a beginning, middle and end".

> "Not all poetry belongs on stage. Some is meant to be read," says Jens. "I chose the poems in ABOUT ANNE because each one of them was a confessional. Something happens in each poem. I was dealing with the 'nownesss' of each poem. I was dealing with the 'nowness' onstage that moves us from one place to another and gives me something to play. An action to play. Every one of the poems shows us this woman at another level of 'aliveness'."

Here's the story Salome Jens tells about her "compelling reason" to work on the Sexton poetry:

> "Hank Hoffman brought the material to me when the LAAT (Los Angeles Actors Theatre) was still at their Oxford Street space in Hollywood. He thought I would be interested but I wasn't so sure. Then he asked me to a performance they were doing of the poems in which he was performing–or reading, really—Anne's work. It was at a woman's prison. I was very impressed with the women who watched and how moved they were by Anne's journey as a wife and mother. It was as hard as their journey. They got that.

The other half of the program was the TRANSFORMATION[18] poems, which had already been snatched up. Someone else had the rights in perpetuity. So, it looked like we couldn't do the main part of the evening and I went away and that was that.

But I went home, went on with my life, and lived with the poems for the next couple of years and they kept haunting me—they were in my head and my heart. I understood them. There were so many things about Anne that mirrored my own experience. I began to feel her crawling inside my veins."

For Jens, the need to do the play and feel the language in her mouth emerged because of a deep identity with the poet. When I approached PICNIC IN EDEN, my poetry play, I too was concerned about writing "events". And finding a "compelling reason" to proceed with this project.

It was slightly different for me. Events coincided in my life that were so enormous, I could not encapsulate them in prose. It is said that in musical plays, the best songs emerge from the text when words no longer serve the emotion of the moment. It is the same in poetry. Poetry in a play emerges when the emotion being presented transcends prose.

I was in my early thirties, unmarried, and unemployed. Like most women of my age, I was looking for an anchor, a home, a relationship, and a career that supported me rather than me supporting it. I read a wonderful biography of writer Elizabeth Bowen in which she said:

"It is not only our fate, but our business to lose innocence. And once we have lost that, it is futile to attempt a picnic in Eden."

Here was the title I wanted. The conflict was evident. The loss of innocence vs. the desire to remain a child and be cared for. These were the issues with which I was dealing. I needed to go on a PICNIC IN EDEN and see how it felt.

Looking for an anchor, I had gotten myself pregnant by mistake and had no way to support a child. Normal sentences could not describe my confusion, unhappiness, surprise and loss. Here is the first thing that came:

JOEY AND THE JOYRIDE

I liked Joey. He had everything
 horn-rimmed and puffing,
his pipe in a white gloved hand gesturing across the
Columbia campus. He was old and wise and full of
commandments.

I was eighteen but when I came to New York
he took me out anyway to Rumplemayer's and
the Russian Tea Room on his father's
expense account which also paid for his pipe tobacco.

Just past $49.99 he consulted his diary and
decided it was time for pay back.
"Ready yourself, grow up, yield. I go to Columbia
My parents are both lawyers.
Your dad worked in the circus, didn't he?
A clown? I'll pick you up at seven."

His dorm room had a slab cot.
A grey army blanket. Fluorescence fluttered
Against sink, mirror, towel rack. Prison toilet.
Abortionist's razor.

He entered the room, right hand first. Flick.
Off the overhead. Black light from across the hall
pulsed to Jimi Hendrix.
His bones clicked against the linoleum.

"Move over. I'm cold," said he.
I did. He lay above, limp and furious.
All dry below decks.
"Come on!" he said. I did what I could.
Sandpaper against cement.

Ooh, he was angry.
"How am I supposed to get hard! You have to help me."
"I don't like you."
"Tell it to the judge."

94

"I don't like this".
"Then, leave. Bitch."

Three AM and cold on the corner
of 117th and Broadway.
The dime in my pocket
wouldn't reach my Dad in Detroit.

"I don't care," I said. "You're stupid."
He pressed against my acetate panties
and his front grew thick.
"There," he sighed. "Now."

His hand reached for his foil packet.
His teeth tore it open. His hands
Busy elsewhere on his own body.
He sheathed himself.

I was cut open.
Prick, drip, done.
Finished.
Oh.

The boy raped me with his pipe and
his manner and my own white gloves.
And I, out of respect for the expectations, allowed it
Could he be wrong? I right? Both fucked?

I saw him holding the sagging white balloon
with his semen and heard him order me
out of his sight. I noted the passing
of a first and last time.

Ten years later, pregnant, unable to
have the child, the first image that came—
that long hallway
in the dorm at Columbia.
And as clear as day,
a cat dragged a piece of filthy wedding lace
down the hall and round the corner. Out of sight
far, far out of reach.

PICNIC IN EDEN
©1980, Susan Merson

95

My memory of this date rape informed the sadness I felt having an unwanted pregnancy. I needed to look at my own sense of power in the world vis a vis men and relationships. I needed to do that right NOW because I had gotten myself into a life changing situation and I didn't realize how or why I had arrived there. A compelling reason and an event that was so enormous that it needed to be condensed so that it could unpack itself, one image at a time, over time.

The poem also occurs in a real place. One can describe and 'inhabit' the restaurants described and the dreaded college dorm room with its slab cot. The hallway is visual and can be created by the actor when onstage. Joey himself can be created from the puffing pipe, to the money diary and the camel hair coat. All these details of character and place create a picture. The details make the people actable and the place itself, alive and "playable".

THE ARC OF THE POETRY PLAY
In this poem, which opened the piece, I set up the young girl, holding onto innocence and the rules that she has been taught. She was polite. She was respectful. She was looking for a good match, a man who would take care of her, as she had been instructed. But by following those rules learned at her mother's knee, this girl got herself raped. By tossing off the advice of a sheltered childhood, she could have defended herself and avoided a painful lesson. But that tossing off the yoke, and assuming adulthood was the arc of the play. I was going to take the audience on the journey.

The arc of Salome Jens' play happened organically as well.

> "I followed the chronology of her (Sexton's) life and every piece fell into place. The arc was her journey through loving and losing and mothering and then the asylum."

QUESTIONS TO PONDER:
What events are you dealing with that can best be explored in the density of poetry?
Can you fashion an event into a concentrated snapshot that is both theatrical and evocative of the event and emotion of your main character? Do images, pictures, emerge organically for you when thinking about this form of monologue?
Can these pictures be made active and connect one to the other to create a forward movement in your piece?

PICNIC IN EDEN moved along to the climax, which was the actual day of the abortion. Here, notice that the language becomes nervous and defensive, allowing the main character to hide her real feelings of isolation and fear. The punctuation of the speech with the languorous names of the beautiful girls all there to have abortions, provides an opportunity for the actress to play with the subtext of the piece, which is the longing for a simpler, less stark time in her life.

THE ROCKER

I mean, you walk into this huge office building on
Park Avenue. I mean, like Park Avenue and
you pass the front security guards and the businessmen
in their three piece suits and carefully placed briefcases
and you go up to the twelfth floor and you're trying to be
nonchalant. I mean, no business suit nonchalant. On Park
Avenue where you don't want to blow it, you know.
And the elevator lurches at every floor and you get there
without heaving and you walk in and
there are all these women.

I mean, all these women. A hundred maybe more
and it's just eight in the morning and they're sitting against
the walls, the long walls in plastic chairs under fluorescence
that makes them green. Kind of. Greenish. Cecilia and Kim
Anandamaia, Lucille and Eloisa Marie.

And there are Rudolph Nureyev and Mihail Baryshnikov
smiling down from the wall in the area where they tell you
about birth control, again, and just what's gonna happen, again,
and the Formica tables are very shiny
with magazines and boxes and boxes and boxes of Kleenex
half used, all the women against the wall.

They are some of them black, some Puerto Rican tan and
some Asian olive and some plain old white bread and spongy.
They call the women one by one. Softly. Nicely.
By their first names Marisol, Adelaida, Monika.
All names carefully chosen for them by their mothers and
those calling the names knowing this and
calling them beautifully, delicately
with great care. You know. It was nice, motherly somehow."

The piece goes on to describe the day. The going and coming, into and out of the waiting room. The faces of the people waiting for the people who are getting rid of the unwanted people. The boredom, the terror and the politics and then the peace offers the lesson learned.

> "The clinic, thank you very much
> Pinpointed the day of conception.
> After a fight at a birthday bed and breakfast
> in Cape May. They let me in on no secret.
> I knew the moment he came.
>
> Fire and gush and ether enveloped us
> dead to sleep for hours
> awaking with a hangover, and he triumphant
> knowing he had been felt
> and me knowing. I had been had."

PICNIC IN EDEN
©1981, Susan Merson.

It finally ends that night, after the event at a movie theatre where moonfaced little children on the screen haunt the teller's dreams.

THE ACTOR MAKES THE DIFFERENCE

The poem must be slick enough, have a broad enough "public surface" to be able to engage the viewer first time through. The actor must embody the basic personality behind the poem in her performance. There must be a real and true connection between the essential action of the poem and the actor who performs or becomes it. It is not enough to sing song the lines—as some famous poets have done in simply reading their work for the public. Instead, the actor must take it one step further and embody the action, define the character expressed in the poem and become the vehicle of understanding for the audience.

If the writer and the actor are the same person, it may be easier. The Actor does know the Writer intimately. But, too intimately to portray the Writer well? A balancing act helped by the Director as discussed in an earlier chapter is probably needed. Phew. A tall order. How do you make these poems with their multiple, dense images, understood?

Specificity. Make clear, bold and connected acting choices.

QUESTIONS TO PONDER:
 Who are you?
 Where are you?
 What are you saying?
 Who are you talking to?
 What do you want from them?
 And why are you saying it?

It is the same in any play for an actor but in a poetry play, this must be even stronger. The words are concentrated and so must be your commitment to the words.

WHO IS THE WRITER? WHO IS THE MAIN CHARACTER?
When we read a poem, we are treated to the voice and viewpoint of the writer. When an actor performs a poem, the actor then becomes the personification of the writer. The actor must then look at the poem differently than the listener or reader might. The actor must study the observation of the writer and then decide what kind of person would make that observation.

When she embarked upon her exploration of Anne Sexton, Salome Jens discovered that:

> "Anne liked to do her poetry to rock bands. She was not a quitter. This was a woman passionate to live. Knowing this gave me a way in. I could perform the play onstage as a solo piece because, of course, I wasn't alone. I was with Anne. She and I knew something and I put her words in my mouth and I said them."

The meaning of a poem can completely change depending on who is saying it. In putting together a play full of poems, one needs to identify the speaker first, and see if the speaker is dynamic and interesting enough to bring to life. Her journey—her action—will be the arc to the piece.

QUESTIONS TO PONDER:
 What does your observation tell us about the writer?
 If the writer is you, do you have enough distance t o create a stage persona?
 If you are compiling a piece by another poet, what do you have in common with the poet that compels you to bring her to life?

Where does the poet live in you?
In the language of the poem?
In the event of the poem?
In the poet's life experience or in what the poet chooses to
write about?

Jens decided that she would play Sexton reciting her poems. This
choice gave the poems an intimacy, a connection and a depth. By
adding the extra layer of being the actual poet giving these words to
the world, the poems became a play. There was conflict and an arc.
Sexton came to tell us something, the poems gave us the story, and
they expressed her inner conflict and then her utter resignation to the
world. The poems became the play because of the glue that the actress
provided.

Jens, again:

> "I 'essenced' it to such a degree. I got down to the very
> concentrated core. My job is to 'essence' the material and
> then give it back to you, the audience. I understood the source
> where she (Sexton) was coming from. The actor says—
> quoting Einstein—'there is nothing human that is alien to
> me'. As an actor I say there is nothing that comes from this
> woman that is alien to me."

WHO IS THE POET?
So, when approaching poetry as a performance text, how does one
"essence" it? Get to its root. As discussed, the first step is to discover
the main character of your play, the writer of the poem. We discover
the character of the writer as we would discover any other character.
We look at behavior, life choices and the language the character—
that is, the poet—chooses to use.

> SMITTY
>
> My heart was aching
> so much
> I engaged the counsel of Smitty
> the Black van man.
>
> He told me
> how he'd run from a woman
> once. "Oh yes."

100

he laughed. "Yes. Ma'am!
She was hard love comin' in buckets.
Watch out brother!"

From PICNIC IN EDEN
©1981-Susan Merson

Smitty, the van man, chose words that revealed his character easily. The writer responded to his frank and down to earth encapsulation of love affairs. We get to know the writer because of the choices she makes in listening to the speaker and choosing to write about the speaker in relation to herself.

The contrast between the two characters creates a conflict—an event—and allows the poems to connect on what Lawrence Ferlinghetti calls "the public surface." That surface is the place most accessible to the listener.

Alternatively, character subtext can be revealed through poetry. A beautiful Ethiopian woman, talking about waiting for her lover in the lobby of the Hilton hotel in Tel Aviv, gives this speech from my play, BOUNTY OF LACE, in which she counsels a young woman against depending too much on a man. We have the character defined. Now we are using the poetry to further define her—by the choice of her words—but also, expose the private world in which she operates.

KITZY

We used to meet on Tuesdays at 3 before he went home
to his wife and drizzly nosed children. There at the Hilton,
full of American tourists and arms dealers
in the lounge making plans to transfer Ketusha missiles to the
vaults of Cairo in exchange for a donation to the Jewish
National Fund.

And I waited at my usual spot with a red drink with vodka
and he never came
As Zubin Mehta flirted with me at the bar
and photojournalists waited for
an interview with Fatah leaders
And the women of Baltimore Hadassah
bought menorahs in the hotel gift shop.

I strolled to the pool and began to sweat.
And he never came.

With my legs soggy and strange
I felt an odd exhilaration, a celebration of secrecy.
I took my gorgeous self up the stairs and
down the hall and slipped the key in
and turned down the bed, sprinkled the rose petals
and drew my bath and sniffed the lavender.
And I have a secret for you

Sex in hotel rooms is better had alone,
amid fantastical lovers who caress
your stomach with cream
and soft lights
and shadows from silk scarves
thrown wantonly across a lamp.

Sex in hotel rooms is mostly in the mind of the beholders,
in the rich mahogany of the bed posts
and the full counted cotton sheets
and the breeze
from the window. And the silence
of the hallways.
the rich carpet beneath bare feet.

I pace the room like a tiger until his image
returns to me
free
So free.

I anoint myself with oils—
high above the city,
in a cool box filled
with the heat of my own dreams
and the sly wink of the room service waiter as
I conjure God at my pleasure
every Thursday at 3 PM.

And no one is the wiser.

It is my own dream
it gives me comfort,

oh my women
ye rams, ye damsels
shower me with raisins and drip honey from the rock
For I am sick of love.

This speech allows the subtext to emerge through the images. It "unpacks" itself fact by fact, sensual delight after stolen moment. In that way, it is an example of poetry as defined by poet Wyatt Prunty. Remember, he says that "poetry complicates things. And then unpacks its meaning, one image after the other."

The other thing about this speech is that it, too, is an event. Each poem onstage must be an action, an event that moves the play along from piece to piece. We move with the character KITZY from the lobby of the hotel, to the silent hallway, to the room, to her individual celebration.

In creating the evening of Anne Sexton poetry that Salome Jens performed, she found this poem, THE PLAY, that completed both the arc of the play she was presenting, and connected actor and subject beautifully. Sexton created a poem that uses the theatrical metaphor that expressed Jens life as much as her own. She was lucky that Jens found her work and so completely identified with it. And Jens took her cue from the poet—the symbiotic relationship continuing—and found just the right material to introduce the audience to the arc of Sexton's life as expressed in her work.

SLAM/RAP POETRY
I would be remiss if I failed to mention slam and rap poetry as part of the solo performance phenomenon. The energy and dynamism of rap artists has fascinated our culture and we are all captivated by the power of the form. There are a few things that give this performance art its own category quite apart from the poetic material discussed above.

Most rap poetry is performed and defined as a song. Rap artists are considered musical artists and their performances are considered concerts. Language, yes, but driven by the beat and the force of personality of the performer. Though the material they present is rhymed and in a "poetic" form, it is, for me, more of a political cri de coeur than a complete poetic event. Rap reveals character but more potently reveals a political agenda. The words in rap or slam are equal to its rhythm and performance energy. The words, it could be argued, are not as important as its rhythm and vitality. Does it, then, qualify as performance art? Probably. Performance and spectacle.

Here is what Playwright Jan Quackenbush says about this:

"... in theatre, the whole dramatic effort is generally aimed to reveal character, when poetry is used (in theatre) it is to effect that aim. Theatricality is another thing altogether, is considered spectacle—like the chandelier that falls in the recent production of Phantom of the Opera. Rap, it seems to me, in a dramatic or theatrical sense, is more 'spectacle', in its use of rhythmic beats and emphatic rhyme schemes."

I am not a rap artist but you may be. Don't dismiss the vitality of this form but make sure it is in the proper arena. Decide for yourself if rap is music, theatre, or a combination of both and then proceed to build your evening. Some may characterize rap performance as doing "Shakespeare with a beat". If it moves you and makes a story, go for it!

As in any solo performance, the construction of the material is extremely personal and must be connected to not only the message but also the messenger. Know thyself. And Know how Thy wants to make thyself heard!

---

**Footnotes:**

—Page 93—
[18] Jens is referring to Sexton's book of reworked fairy tales, TRANSFORMATIONS.

## ELEMENTS OF THIS FORM

### POETRY IN THEATRE REVEALS CHARACTER

Poetry is a great form to use when the emotion you are discussing is too big for normal language. It reveals the inside and the outside of feeling. Character is language, image and silence.

### THE ACTOR IS THE GLUE

In a poetry play, the actor creates the glue and dynamism of character that moves the story forward. The actor is real and solid, not an image. Therefore, the audience looks to the actor to define the world in a way they can understand.

### SAIL ON THE LANGUAGE

Sometimes just the sound and rhythm of a word can do the work of communicating to an audience for you. Don't over act. Respect the language and its power.

### CREATE YOUR ARC

Same rules apply here as in any play. There must be a compelling reason to write and perform the piece. The must be an arc—a beginning, a middle that conflicts and changes the direction, and an ending a resolution. Remember the Alice Walker quote that any short story is as easy as ABDCE—ACTION, BACKGROUND, DEVELOPMENT, CLIMAX, ENDING,

### DEFINE THE EVENT OF EACH POEM

We recognize conflict by contrasting the voice of the writer with the character's he describes in his poem. We recognize "event" by what happens in the "nowness" of each poem.

# NOTES:

Susan Merson as Hippie Daughter in FAMILY SECRETS
Credit: Detroit Jewish News

## V: CLARICE COHEN'S TRIBAL TALES OF LOVE - THE GALLERY OF SUSPECTS: Six Characters in Search of An Event

There was a long hiatus between the construction of PICNIC IN EDEN and the development of CLARICE. Time intervened and brought me a new life in California, a daughter, a husband and many more responsibilities. My career began to change with the locale, the marketplace and all of the sudden I looked around and realized that I was no longer an ingénue. A wonderful feeling, believe me. It was great to no longer have the angst of romance or the desperate desire to please. If you're not there yet, hold on. It gets better.

Working in television and film gives one many new skills but for the everyday working actor in Los Angeles, the job is primarily fulfilling visual expectations. One strives to become the perfect looking lawyer, or the most intelligent doctor look-alike. I have played the role of a different "Dr. Klein" on at least ten major television dramas and though I consider myself a thoughtful and accomplished actress, the only real difference between all these women was the color of the doctors coat, and the length of my hair at the time. Too often, I prepared for auditions thinking about the color of my blouse on camera or whether or not my glasses would telegraph the right choice for the slot to a casting director who may not even have been born when I started out as an actress. Ah well.

RECONNECTED
I was lucky enough to land the role of Aunt Gert in the film of Neil Simon's LOST IN YONKERS and reconnect to my character acting roots. This poor woman had a terrible breathing disorder called dysphonia that caused her to speak on an intake of breath as her anxiety increased. Despite her breathing problem, she had a great deal of dignity and real courage. It was a wonderful challenge to find a way

to make her real enough to withstand the prying eye of a camera close-up.

I enjoyed Gert. She reminded me of where I came from. She was a simple, earnest woman getting through her little life with heroic fortitude. There were lots of women like that in my life. A large circle of aunts and cousins had likewise sustained enormous humor and self-esteem despite formidable barriers. They, like Gert, just got their lives done and wasted no time on complaints. I enjoyed the opportunity to play a real woman with a history. Not a babe, but a woman of a certain age who every day became, as Emily Dickinson said, "not older with years but newer every day".

I looked around and realized that many of the people that I had grown up with in the theatre no longer looked the way they did a generation before—but still had the same passion. Just like Gert.

In the film and television business, one goes from ingénue to the grave in a half of a breath. One day you're starring on a sitcom as a young bride at age 30 and the next season you're cast as a grandmother—at age 31. There is no longevity, especially for women, since the market is focused on making money. The demographic that buys the products that are advertised on television, and who go to the mainstream movies, is age 12 to 33 years old. I guess the rest of us don't count for much.

I began to see my "compelling reason" for the next piece to emerge. One, to demonstrate that women do not die at age 30 and two, to remind myself that theatrical and complex characters have a place in the theatre. There was a way to explore passion past age fifty! Could there be such a thing?

I had heard a National Public Radio story about a middle-aged Jewish woman who had sent her last kid off to college and began to moonlight as a singer at a small local restaurant in Great Neck, New York. The woman was a tireless self-promoter and soon had a following for which she played at every senior center and nursing home in her tri-state area. She was the queen of the nursing home circuit.

At about the same time there was an article in the paper about a suburban man of 79 years old who had strangled his wife of 60 years and when asked why he did it, he responded that she "coughed too much". Ah ha! My mind began to whirr. What could cause such a ruthless act? Hardening of the arteries perhaps—or misdirected passion! I chose the latter motivation and the story of Clarice—a woman who wouldn't quit, and Ernie Abrams—a man who snapped and murdered his wife—began to take shape.

Jan Lewis, Artistic Director of the Jewish Women's Theatre Project in Los Angeles, asked me to put these ideas together and come up with something for her Festival of Plays for the New Millennium at the Skirball Cultural Center. This was the fourth element that created a "compelling reason".

CHARACTER VERSUS STORY
Right at the beginning of this project, the challenges began to emerge. I was interested in how all these elements came together in one cohesive story. I wanted to tell a story, rather than explore one character as I had in CHINA DOLL. I wanted to have a throughline that served as a prism, each character revealing another side of the central story. I had never done this by creating a world where everyone had their own Roshomon version of the universe and I wanted to move toward that end.

Was I to create this play via story or via character? Clarice was rich. Very emotive. Larger than life and so much fun to play. Should she tell us everything? She was pretty hard to contain. Let me introduce you to her.

> A SPOT COMES UP STAGE RIGHT PLATFORM. SILHOUETTED AGAINST A SMOKY BLUE DROP IS CLARICE COHEN, MID 60'S, MIDLIFE CHANTEUSE. SHE WEARS BLACK SEQUINS, HER HEAD IS THROWN BACK AS SHE SINGS

> CLARICE (SINGING)

> NEVER KNOW HOW MUCH I NEED YA
> NEVER KNOW HOW MUCH I CARE
> WHEN I PUT MY ARMS AROUND YA
> I GETTA FEVER—OY I JUST DON'T CARE
> YOU GIMME FEVER—IN MY KISHKES
> FEVER ALL THRU MY SPINE
> FEVER! CAN I RISK YA? C'MON NOW—LET'S DRINK SOME WINE

111

(OH MANIZCHEWITZ) FEVER! LET US DRINK SOME WINE!

TEPID APPLAUSE. A NASAL
VOICE ON P.A.

(VO ANNOUNCER)
We thank Mrs. Cohen for entertaining the residents of Mt. Misnah so beautifully once again! Thank you Mrs. Cohen and remember, residents, tuna sandwiches ready and waiting in the activities room. B taer von!

CLARICE'S THEME SONG "I DID
IT MY WAY" IS HEARD AS THE
SPOT GOES DOWN ON HER
AND LIGHTS UP ON HER
DRESSING TABLE. SHE ENTERS
HER DRESSING ROOM.

SHE MOVES TO A TRIPOD WITH
A VIDEO CAMERA MOUNTED
ON IT. TURNS IT ON. SMILES
GRACIOUSLY AND BEGINS. DO
WE SEE HER ON SCREEN AS
SHE TALKS?

Don't you just love my home away from home? I wasn't always quite so boheme. Up until a few years ago, I was content with my lifetime temple membership at Temple Beth Isaiah courtesy of my late husband. But I soon realized that I needed MORE when my Irwin died and that part of my life was over...

I'd always loved the theatre. I went to Barnard. Did I mention that? Irwin was an engineer. We moved to the suburbs. I had three children. They were terrific. One got married. One got divorced. One spent time in an ashram with a mishuganah guru. I judge not. I only say I breathe a mother's sigh of relief that my children have finally found their own path. And if they find resonance in a mix of cabala and animal sacrifice, I cannot judge...for they are grown...flown...their own people...and now there is my life to live. I can wait no more!

This tour opened originally at the Village Boite. The club in Lenny Cantrowitz's strip mall? Not far from the Galleria? Perhaps you know it. Next to the Mailboxes, ETC? Good parking...Ah, Lenny owed Irwin...and me...but that's another story. We opened, we hit, and the rest is history.

We have been on the road for months...26 weeks to be exact...and what can I say? It's a wonderful life! I've always wanted to sing the classics...the songs that come from my heart, my kishkes...

MUSIC SWELLS
CLARICE SINGS

"I'VE GOT A RIGHT TO SING THE BLUES!
I'VE GOT A RIGHT TO FEEL LOW DOWN"

TAPED APPLAUSE CHEER HER
EFFORTS. SHE PUNCHES HER
OWN BOOM BOX FOR
ACCOMPANIMENT
APPLAUSE.

A preview of the next album, available by mail order very soon.

Ernie Abrams was the last man I thought I would fall for. Especially after Irwin who was such a...a provider. But Ernie had that certain something. He really grabbed me at that temple mixer. He grabbed me, we rhumba-ed, I felt my life spring back into my veins. Estelle, his wife, just sat there. She did nothing while Ernie and I cha cha-ed around the room, and she sat there—staring, her big google eyes behind those horrible glasses she never even wiped. Some called her regal. I called her ruined.

Anyway...Ernie and I...we had a little affair...And then it grew and grew into a grand passion and for the first time in years I managed to feel my heart again and my knishes and my tuches...and I felt hungry, hungry and hungry for this man and his, frankly, shriveled private parts that for me were like jewels on the banquet table.

We made love at every Holiday Inn that had a senior discount. Ernie is a bit older than me and we had this wonderful weekend at the new Holiday Inn—just opened off the 405—(I think Estelle, his wife, was with their daughter, Mae. Heavy set girl...down in Florida for a week.) We had this weekend nestled in the hills and I was in heaven.

And then he told me. He told me that he could never get free. Estelle would never let him go. That I was forever condemned to the role of the lover...never to be respected...always to be slightly tawdry...on the outside like Stella Dallas...always on the outside looking in...

I left our love nest dejected, subdued but then, as the days went by I saw my dream dissolving and I went nuts. I lost control...and I knew that they partook of the senior special luncheon at the top of the May Company every Wednesday afternoon. I would not be tossed aside as yesterdays hash!!!

 I had a gun...it was a beebee gun...not a real gun...just a starter pistol from an unfortunate music video but I could not stop myself. I went to the May company. I knew they were having the fish special and I stood there, tears in my eyes and watched as Ernie shared his pathetic meal with Estelle. They said nothing to each other, they had no chemistry, they had nothing between them! And I took out that pistol and I aimed it at her head and I gave a shry: "ESTELLE! YOU'RE AS GOOD AS DEAD ALREADY! WHY NOT DIE NOW AND LEAVE ERNIE TO A WOMAN WHO CAN REALLY LOVE HIM!" and then I shot the pistol. I shot it. It made a huge noise. Her coffee cup shattered. She flung it at the mirror! It was a mess...fish sticks, carrots, and mayhem!

And Estelle...Estelle! She got very upset, and never was able to swallow again without some horrible burping or the most annoying cough I have ever heard... terrible...keh keh keh...Ernie...keh keh Clarice...keh keh...a person SHOULD die being so unpleasant. Alright, maybe it was me that propelled him to such violence later in this story. But for the moment, Ernie stared at me and Estelle just stared— her glasses dripping with tartar sauce—and did nothing but try to clear her throat.

She moved into her own bedroom after that, refused to sleep with Ernie. And we reconciled.

But it affected him, eventually, her cloistering herself. His manliness was called into question. He became less able to perform with me, started whining about his wife and her cough, and his dilemma. I told him. I said to him, "Erneleh! Don't let your life pass you by! Do something! Extricate yourself from this living hell!" But he would do nothing. Not then at least...and finally...well...finally I left him, too. I needed some sense of a bright tomorrow.

 I went to therapy—Dr. Philip Cantrowoitz, MFCC, PH.D Harvard Medical School, Swiss clinics forever—and learned "I have to sing my own blues." I told Ernie, "I cannot sing yours, my darling." I understand what drove him to it...and if you want my honest opinion…there was a moment when I watched him on court TV…all hunched and bent, sitting there in such shame...there was a moment that my heart wanted to fly to him and sing
OH MY MAN I LOVE HIM SO!


There we go. Irrepressible! And she wanted to keep talking! But, I needed to hear someone else's perspective on the situation. Clarice was such a large personality, her voice may not have been the most trustworthy, especially when it came to the facts of a murder and it's motivation. She could tell us about herself and her world, but could she tell us the whole story? Could she make clear the whole picture with its many sides?

She could if this was the world according to Clarice however; I was attempting to create a larger story that contained this woman and the others that were part of the search for truth.

Had I wanted to tell Clarice's story alone, I would have expanded her monologues and created an overall timeline. Instead I wanted to create a world, and so, I needed to people the world with other opinions and perspectives.

I put the idea of "arc" on hold while I began to let others speak about the murder, explain the facts, complete the picture of both Clarice, the man she loved and the world they all lived in. I asked myself the following questions and came up with answers that created the people who needed to be in this particular world.

How did the media view the murder? I introduced an ineffectual NEWS CASTER.

How crazy was CLARICE? Was she all affect and no substance? I let her DAUGHTER come onstage and try to reach her mom. I let the daughter try to define herself and the woman who raised her.

How affected was ERNIE, the murderer, by his crime? I let Ernie speak for himself of his love for both Clarice and his demanding wife, ESTELLE, who he murdered.

How did ERNIE's action affect what was left of his family? His distressed thirty something daughter, MAE, showed up to gather her mother's remains.

Is there anyone who sees CLARICE as she really is and needs her as a role model? A monologue from Ernie's GRAND DAUGHTER who admires Clarice's panache emerged.

And finally:

What does the murdered woman herself have to say about the situation? And ESTELLE came forth with a bristling admission of guilt in her own murder.

This process helped to create the larger world of these characters. They helped to push the story away from only one person—Clarice— and ask the audience to consider a larger idea about the need for humans to have a sense of purpose and place in the universe. What does it take to stay alive and vital in our contemporary society? What do we need? Love, purpose, passion and place. I was pleased that these characters were helping me to ask larger questions. One by one they opened the world of the main character and gave us context and back-story.

Now I had all these characters but I wasn't sure what brought them together. I had subtext. I knew generally what they were all talking about but I still needed to know and define why they were on the stage together? What did they have to offer each other? I loved them but I got lost in their individual complexities. I got lost in the rich and wild world of each of these characters.

QUESTIONS TO PONDER
When placing more than one character in your solo piece, how do you define their relationship to each other and to the overall arc of the play?
Can you define the difference between the two for yourself and your play?

Stephanie Satie, in developing her solo play, REFUGEES, went through a similar process. Stephanie was teaching English as a Second Language and began to fall in love with her students and their stories. These stories—these characters—"were a dramatic event" that she "longed to get on a stage" but she had to sort through the characters and see how they hung together.

"At the very beginning," says Satie, "I was so blown away by some of the stories, that I either wrote them down, asked them to write short essays or just repeated what I heard. I soon had this bulging folder of stories. I was writing volumes about my family. My students sometimes morphed into family members before my very eyes. I had this enormous amount of stuff. I knew that a dramatic event was taking place every day and that I wanted to put it on stage. I brought it to the Writers Bloc and read this enormous mess to two friends and everyone was blown away by the stories but they didn't quite get the personal stuff (and how it connected with the other material)."

Stephanie was looking for an overall arc that would connect her characters and make them a play. In my case, I, too, had six wonderful characters in search of a plot.

This is a common problem in "GALLERY OF CHARACTERS" solo plays. These evenings have wonderful portraits of diverse folk.

117

The actor has a great time showing her versatility. The audience is dazzled by the performer's virtuosity—but the central event of the evening, the play, can get lost.

There are many of these kinds of plays that do well, but I contend they could do even better if they would pay more attention to what the entire story adds up to rather than the eccentricities of the various characters. In other words, what is the "event"?

I had an opportunity to perform in Sherry Glaser's solo play, FAMILY SECRETS. This is a wonderful gallery of family photographs, loosely connected by the fact that we watch the actress transform in front of the audience and become FATHER, MOTHER, HIPPIE SISTER, PUNK SISTER and GRANDMOTHER. The audiences loved the theatricality of the people. As an actor, it was wonderful to offer such a tour de force, but as an actress performing the play—rather than a writer/performer bringing to life my family, it became clear that there was no central arc that I was playing.

When I did it, I was just showing off my versatility. When Sherry did it, she was making a more profound statement about her own family and evolution as a woman. The arc of the play, the event of FAMILY SECRETS is "look at how I unfurl before you. I am standing here and all of these people are part of me." The fact that SHE—SHERRY was there in person revealed something about her. She changed as an actress and as a person. There was no actual language that defined her as character. Her personal presence was the arc that held these characters in place. As with the drama of Anne Frank, when Sherry Glaser performed her play it worked because the conflict was between herself and the world that she created. When I, another actress—another layer removed from the compelling reason for the piece—got into the act, the play lost its punch. It was six portraits but told the audience little about why they were all in one place at one time. The gallery of characters did not add up to a play with a central "perception shift" when I did it. The audience learned nothing about the central character, the Actress. There was no story with a beginning, middle and end. It was a random series of interviews of interesting people who were in the same family and that was that.

Stephanie Satie found a connection between the characters she was presenting in developing herself—the teacher—as an independent character that held the rising action of the play.

"The impact the stories were having on the Teacher was increasing with every draft. It was becoming inescapable."

This made her uncomfortable. She wanted the play to be about the students.

"In my mind, originally it was their story and only theirs. 'This isn't about me; it's about them' was my mantra. Early on, Anita (my director Anita Khanzadian) kept prodding me. She kept asking me 'how does this affect you…?' It became clear that this was the teacher's journey and about this dynamic relationship in the classroom and how it changed the Teacher's (my) perspective on my own family of immigrants. I realized that this was the throughline—that's when it became a play."

With CLARICE I was so caught up in showing aspects of character that I needed to go back to make sure there was an event to the play, a central event and central character who changed. The first time I performed the play, the arc was buried too deeply.

I knew there was a problem after the brief Los Angeles run and consulted my longtime friend and colleague, Curt Dempster, the Artistic Director of Ensemble Studio Theatre in New York. He nailed the problem right away. There was no ticking clock driving the action forward and there was no central event—in the present—that was consuming the characters as we meet them. Each character spoke from their own reality but it had no affect on the other people in the play. I needed to find the ARC of the piece and offer a mystery to the audience that they would be willing to sit and try to solve.

After the Los Angeles premiere of the piece, I went back to it and restructured it. Curt suggested that each of the characters is waiting for the verdict. Will Ernie get the chair, get released or end up in a mental institution? Each monologue should happen chronologically and each time a person speaks, we move closer to knowing what will happen to Ernie and those that are affected by him. The question we are waiting to have answered is whether Ernie will be sentenced to death for Estelle's murder or not. The central character, Clarice, is a different person at the end of the play than she was in the beginning because of the affect of this event upon her personality.

Each character addresses that central question. Will Ernie live or die because of his crime? Should he live or die? How will his fate affect mine (as the character)? How will Clarice be changed?

And with each monologue, we need to keep the ticking clock going. That means that in each monologue, we need to move closer to a decision.

Here is how the timeline arc worked in the play:

> CLARICE MONOLOGUE #1- Night before the sentencing, Clarice gives us background but also sets up tension and central question—what will happen to Ernie and, by inference, herself? Will her lover be put to death and is she responsible in some way?

> CLARICE'S DAUGHTER-News of the impending sentencing hits the national airwaves on the morning news shows. Character reveal gives us more information about Clarice but also tells us where we are in terms of time and how this is affecting people across the country.

> ERNIE- Awaiting the sentencing in his cell, his anxiety grows as does ours. I used images of the sun being high in the sky letting us know that it was midday and we still hadn't heard. Here, the language of the play became more poetic and more urgent as his sense of desperation increased, driving us through this middle point of the play.

> ERNIE'S DAUGHTER, MAE- Mae comes back to her parents' apartment to await the word. We see a person defeated by her parents, and we set up the place where the word will come down. Shadows are beginning to lengthen. We know the end of the day is hastening. Mae speaks to her erstwhile boyfriend, increasing the sense of helplessness felt by everyone. Here is the preparation, the battening down of the hatches, so to speak.

> ERNIE'S GRANDDAUGHTER- is in a hotel in Jersey with her boyfriend who has run out on her. The boyfriend wants to know if her grandfather will be determined crazy or a murderer. He doesn't want to father a child who has a great grandfather who is a murderer. "She's fucking weird enough already, dude." The television is on in the motel room. The pizza delivery guy interrupts her. It is already 9 PM in the east.

CLARICE- orders dinner in California but can't eat as the "agita" is consuming her. She is still waiting and putting on a brave "On With the Show" face. We learn more about final details. She makes a decision to go to Ernie's apartment to watch television and await the answer on Ernie's fate. CLARICE's anxiety increases and she can't get her key in the door. She stands frustrated and caught in the hallway. Upset by all the noise,

ESTELLE- the murdered wife appears as a very angry ghost. She speaks her piece and essentially it is Estelle who passes judgment on Ernie, rather than the courts. She is climax of the piece. Listen.

                    ESTELLE, WEARING THE RED DRESS IN WHICH SHE SEDUCED ERNIE APPEARS FROM THE DEAD.

ESTELLE

OK. OK, STOP. STOP IT NOW... You hear me! Stop it! All right. That's it. I have been on the Other Side listening to you and your "friends". It's too much noise! Love is not a bad thing, it's just something I was never very good at— Look, I hold nothing against Ernie. I was greedy... I wanted everybody on hold until I decided to love...it can drive a man crazy. That's what happened. Don't believe anybody else's theories...

And ESTELLE proceeds to explain how she got to the bitter woman she was and how Ernie should not be held accountable for a murder, which, from her point of view was a favor.

Did I ever tell you what happened in my grandfather's bedroom in Poland? With the brown postcards on a string advertising Palestine and his dream? How he used to do crazy magic things in that room. Blow gas? Eat garlic? Stink and pray? Never ate candy.

My grandmother made pickles in the kitchen. My Zedah hid them in his pocket and ate them with herring right there on

121

the clean white sheets while he stuffed my head with the Talmud, the Torah, Maimonides, Shulchan Aruch and on and on and on... he had these tiny pickles and they'd stick out and he'd always ask me. Try a pickle, Essele? A teeny pickle? He had an ancient sewing machine in the corner of the room. "Pickles from my pocket, Essele?" He'd offer me. I'd never touch. But I'd feel something... Deep, deep inside...something that I was afraid would eat me crunchy—like when my Grandfather ate the pickles with his enormous yellow teeth.

I'd cry to my Bubbe in the kitchen to keep me from him and she'd say to me: "Go with your Zedah, Essele. He is a wise and good man. Go with your Zedahle."

And I would go back into his bedroom and hide in the closet and try to fall asleep. Crouched behind the sewing machine in the shadows of the bedroom, I swear, there were spirits. Goat boys and little dybbuks who danced with their legs spread and pupiks dangling and they grabbed at my spouting breasts with nasty giggles. Their little schvanzes jumping out at me, licking me with their green tongues! Fiery spit dripping from their fingers. I was so terrified. Never at rest. But once I went inside that room there was no coming out. Bubbe never ever rescued me. She never disturbed her husband in his den. I was caught like a cheese in a mousetrap.

Three musty brown suits hung above me. Shadows were quilted on his brown wooden bed and my Zedah would surround me with his dreams—of the Talmud—of the commentaries of Rashi and Rambam. It was Zedah who decided to tell me of the laws of purity and cleanliness.

"Do you know, Essele, the days that a woman is unclean? Do you know?"
I was 11 years old! My body was just beginning to flower!
"Do you know, Essie, how the Shekhina will wrap you in her arms and squeeze you til the breath drips from you in fiery pools!"
And the Shekhina did dance on my shoulder as Zedah fell into rapture.

The Shekhina, the female part of God, her talons, pierced me, violated me! She blew smoke in my ears as my grandfather's yellow breath clattered and shrouded the room. A dervish of Poland and sweat and wool! And I felt the Shekhina inside of me! All alone in that room! I felt her! She had crawled within and there was blood on my leg!

I screamed and my Bubbe finally came. She finally came and saw it—to rescue me from him, I thought, from the blood, I thought, but no! She came up to me and she lifted her hand and she slapped my face and she said "Mazel Tov. Today you are a woman!"

I couldn't catch my breath. I felt like I was being tongued by God and my Grandfather screaming at me: "God is a vengeful God!"
"Bubbe, save me," I said. And she was making pickles in the kitchen! "Bubbe save me!" And I was shivering and covered in spit.
"Bubbe save me! Mama save me!" And nobody came.

That night they took me to the rabbi. They told him I was a woman and he shook his head. He spoke in many tongues and told me of the power of God and how I would always be safe in the Torah. He spoke of the treasures of womanhood, of my sensual brown arms and his lingering eyes and he spoke of God's fierceness and told me that he saw how I suffered—caught now, drowning in talesim and caught by the leather straps of the tefillin. But he wrapped me tighter.

And as he spoke of this to me, I began to feel my skin being peeled from my flesh. It made me start like a blind colt fighting against the rope.

And then he spoke of the responsibility God places on women to be "frutiful and multiply" and I watched him transfixed and nodded my head to shake the tears from my eyes. He spoke to me of having Jews to populate the land of Palestine, to make sure that the enemies of the Jews would never win because there would be too many of us for them to burn.

And he spoke of the holiness of prayer, the holiness between a man and a woman and how the cabala queen—the Shekhina—searches for these sparks of sex between man and woman and how these sparks were the matter of the world

123

and how our children are our holy sparks and how we must give ourselves over to the task of holy infants and as he spoke, I felt myself being elevated on a golden dais and draped round in purple satin and my doltish shmattes fell away and I was annointed with rubies and emeralds and sheets of satin and cascades of silk and I rose above them in the rabbi's study and
they could see my belly begin to protrude and tiny feet and toes begin to emerge from my vagina and they saw how I could be swimming in children and swimming in children and swimming in children until I drowned. I alone could save the Jewish people.

And the next day I was raped by a Nazi soldier.
And they shot my Bubbe and my Zedah.
And the rabbi and the soldier who defiled himself by poking a dirty Jew.
And I gave birth to a stillborn child.

And my grandmother floated down from the heavens and said, I was not holy enough.
And my mother said, Amen
And my Zedah and my father and the Nazi doctors,
they all said
Amen.
The dead child and I had to find a way to live again.

I never wanted another but Ernie your zaydie… What can we say? He was always such a vigorous man… Athletic—he could never give it up. Always…always...anyway

I gave in to hope. I gave the world another human person on the planet. I replaced the murdered monster that God made me carry long too long ago. I gave forth life...and I told her. Live! Live goddammit! But you can't expect me to help you with it! I haven't the first idea how to live a life... So Live! Go ahead! I dare you!

That is too big a burden for any person to bear. I know. I'm sorry. That's it. That was my time on earth. Now you try.

After that impassioned call from the dead, we realize that Ernie cannot be held responsible for the murder. Estelle was complicitous in her own death. Clarice watches from Ernie's apartment. She is a changed woman by what has happened in the space of the play. She realizes that she was guilty of nothing except trying to love someone. She got out just in time though now she is left bereft but stronger. And there is hope for her future with Ernie now that his ghosts have forgiven him.

GRAPHING THE ARCS

Once I developed this time line, I needed to readjust each monologue to reflect the stakes for each character. What will happen to each of them in relation to the overall story?

I needed to answer the basic questions:

> This is a play about_____?
> The main event of the play is_____?
> How does each character contribute to the central question of the play?
> How does the central character of the play—Clarice—change from beginning to end?

These are the essential questions to be asked with every play. Now put them to your piece and see how you come out?

LAYER CAKE

The development of this gallery of characters play was like a layer cake. First layer is the characters, the second layer is the stakes, and the frosting in the middle is the dramatic question and how it will affect each character. This style of play differs from a compilation play in that it takes on the questions of dramatic unity. The time line is connected and illustrated by each character. The stakes are related to the individual characters and the overall dramatic question.

For Satie, the evolution of her central character of the teacher came from the continued questioning and prodding of a discerning director. As Satie relates:

> "Anita (Khanzadian) kept asking how the women speaking to me affected me. She urged me to write small monologues to the audience and finally to the class itself illuminating my own family and perspective on them. I wrote small pieces still insisting it wasn't about me...until it clicked. Ironically, the audiences came away moved especially by the Teacher's journey, but this glue, this connecting tissue totals probably only three or four minutes, maybe just a little more out of 75 minutes of material.

Each story is the voice of a separate character, set in a different context. And yet the impetus with me is always the same—looking through the keyhole of another, finding the universal in the individual story and of course, my own hunger for stories never ceases. I've shaped myself through others, too."

CLARICE remains the most challenging piece in my repertoire. I experimented with character, with language, with acting styles and genre. Director Randee Trabitz, who did both the reading and workshop production of the piece, moved it masterfully into a "noir" genre that heightened the dark side of each character and their journey. This allowed me as actress to explode with idiosyncratic detail that was wildly entertaining to me if not always to my audience members. With this piece, I chose to "go for broke" and make large choices with language, character and production values.

I chose to incorporate video and music, heightened lighting effects and "campy" acting choices that made the evening a challenge. I felt these choices were right for the piece and for me as an actress at the time but I believe the piece could just as easily have been more "heartwarming" and silly, easier in general to access. I have no regrets about the choices made but I mention them because they were central to the time and place of my artistic exploration.

One of the reasons we do solo pieces must be to challenge ourselves and our audiences as artists. It is fine to do yet another biographical portrait of a famous writer but in making that choice, make sure you know why you are doing the piece and what you want out of it.

MOTIVATION IS ALL
As an actress, I was making a BIG move. I wanted to stretch as wide as I could. I wanted to play a million characters, and sing and make people laugh and cry and sit up and take notice. I wanted it all, just like Clarice and, like Clarice herself, I won a little, lost a little and in the end, learned some painful lessons.

Opening night of the workshop production, I was stretched to my very edges. I had produced the piece, written the piece, consulted on marketing, cleaned the theatre, was running my own box office and I was acting—six characters. Eventually, all the pieces fell together but opening night I was so exhausted I couldn't remember a thing. Literally. The piece was 17 minutes longer than usual. That means there were a lot of—way too many—meaningful pauses. The piece was slow. The audience was overwhelmed and I was unable to buoy them up and lead them through this complex maze that I had created.

I suppose that everyone has had these kinds of opening nights but it doesn't lessen the humiliation. Friends approached with tight smiles and wan faces, and the theatre emptied out quickly. Even my press person fled after the first act curtain and I was left with a disappointed but game director who tried to tell me it "wasn't as bad as it could have been". Silently we munched our baked potatoes and attempted to enjoy the bottle of expensive champagne we had purchased for the occasion. It didn't help. The evening was a mess. I did too much and everyone paid the price.

The lesson here is that if you are going to be a one man band, or in this case—orchestra—make sure someone whacks you, tells you to come to your senses and if you won't, then—makes sure you get the support you need.

Sometimes our desire to get the work done and out into the world overcomes our sense of logic and practicality. That is often a good thing, but in the case of this complex piece, it was not.

CLARICE was a full evening in the theatre. It was more demanding than any previous form of solo performing I had attempted and because of this, it needed another producer beside me. I had my vision and wanted to run with it but I realized I was not SUPERHUMAN. I needed to share my vision and get others on board. It was as important to the project as writing the words and acting the characters.

This form and its production values needed someone else beside me to say YES.

GETTING TO YES IS A TEAM EFFORT
Here is a tough problem. Often we turn to solo performing because we choose to be our own selves onstage. We want our true selves to be presented to the world without constraint. We write our own words, tell our own stories and want the independence of living an artistic life. When this works, it is wonderful but the nature of the theatrical culture in the United States asks that most solo performers are also their own managers.

This is a mixed blessing. It can give us incomparable freedom but it also can weigh us down with too much responsibility, diverting our focus from the work itself and shortchanging our artist selves as well as our audience. And that's just our artistic lives—what about our day to day responsibilities like washing the clothes and making sure peanut butter and jelly—the good kind—is in the pantry closet as promised.

Especially when you are doing a more complex piece, with many characters and technical requirements, be smart about creating a team to support your work. The most magical theatre piece in the world will fail if it is not created with and by a team that believe in the work, or at least are paid to believe in the work. Balance your resources. Make sure the work can sail because you have others helping to lift you airborne, if you need it.

PRODUCER
In previous chapters, I have discussed the need for a good director in developing your projects. As you expand and set your sights on larger game, find a producer that will help you achieve your goals.

There are two kinds of producers. One is a Line Producer who you pay to take care of details. The other is a Producer who reads or sees your work and takes on the production responsibilities and costs.

Both have their advantages. The first is an expense of the Production. The second requires you to share the ownership of your piece. Weigh the possibilities carefully. As discussed previously, during your workshop production it is better to have someone with whom you have a one-year contract. You can re-negotiate after you see whether you have a hit or not.

In doing this form of solo performing and taking responsibility for a more complex artistic vision, you have stepped up to a new level.

Congratulations, but think carefully. You sacrifice the ability to be on your own. You gain the opportunity to work in community. Balance the pros and cons and move forward accordingly.

## ELEMENTS OF THIS PLAY

### COMPELLING CHARACTERS
Let's face it. In this kind of play, you want to offer as much variety as possible so the characters need to be varied, specific and passionate.

### DEFINE A CENTRAL QUESTION
Each character needs to be involved with and helping to answer the central question. Always relate each monologue to moving the story along.

### GRAPH YOUR ARC
How does each character's individual journey within the play build the overall arc of the play? Recognize that the character arc is subservient to the overall arc, and the event of the play. Characters serve the larger universe rather than the other way around. Calibrate the impact of each character with this in mind.

### BUILD YOUR LAYER CAKE
Make sure each character is specific, has personal stakes and contributes to the overall arc.

### DECIDE ON THE COMPLEXITY OF YOUR PRODUCTION VALUES, AND YOUR CHARACTER VALUES.
It is fun to up the ante and create a full production around yourself. Make artistic decisions based on inspiration and then backed up by what is possible—that is, what you can achieve production wise while you stay true to your artistic vision.

### ASSESS YOUR NEEDS
Make sure you have the production support that you need. Reach but be careful not to overreach. The goal is to make the thing work. Decide what "making it work" means to you

129

**NOTES**:

Susan Merson as Mom in FAMILY SECRETS
Credit: Detroit Jewish News

## VI: "HAIR: A REMINISCENCE"- THE SIMPLE NARRATIVE: Storytelling with Heart- Speaking in Your Truest Voice

The complexity of Clarice stopped me in my tracks. I had given that piece my all. I wanted a great deal from it and as usually happens, it—the piece—was not interested in what I wanted from it, but rather it was interested only in what it had to teach me.

It taught me humility. It taught me the Zen value of being with the work rather than with the outcome of the work. It taught me that simplicity and directness are to be understood and valued. It also stopped me from writing for a while.

These breaks in productivity come and are to be tolerated and even nurtured. The flow of work that comes from your subconscious is a tap that needs replenishment and respect. If the work isn't coming, leave the work alone. It will come when it is supposed to come and in the meantime, your job is to live life, work hard, scrub the floor, walk the dog and earn enough to pay the rent. I never liked that kind of advice when it came my way. Alas, the universe has its own agenda and our job is to do the work presented to us. The truth of these quiet periods is that they are the times when we are gathering the next round of material that will eventually be available for us to channel.

As a young actress, discouraged by the difficulty of earning a living and the disrespect with which actors are regarded in our society, I would often dramatically announce that I was giving up my life as an artist. This would usually be followed by tears of desperation, pangs of guilt at the enormous failure I had amounted to and a general emotional mess. Then, I would get some kind of awful day job, remembering the words of the accomplished actress Maureen Stapleton. When asked why she was found selling makeup at a drug store counter, she answered haughtily: "There is no shame in making a living." So, be it.

I sold advertising for a Polish newspaper. I ran business meetings in Acapaulco. I served breakfast at Steak and Brew in Times Square at five in the morning, taking the subway into town from Brooklyn while Eastern European women, wrapped in babushkas, jammed the subway returning home after spending the night cleaning the floors of the huge office buildings in midtown. I hated every one of those jobs. I thought I was destined to a life of drudgery. But guess what? I remember every fold of the babushkas that rode the F train. I remember the feel of the spongy bread served to French tourists and hurled back at me with contempt when I tried to explain this was the best toast America had to offer.

And every time I thought it was over, I realized, that it—this artistic life—cannot be over because it is not something arbitrary that we do or do not do on a whim. We are artists, for better or for worse.

It is a vocation. Like a chronic disease. We are artists because that is who we are and so we need not worry about whether this is true or not. We have nothing to do with this truth. As artists, we will always look at the world a certain way; will always use our skills of observation and emotional recall to connect with the world around us. And we will give the gift, one way or the other, because we have no choice.

OK. So. I wrote Clarice and gave up the theatre. Ha.

I focused on raising my daughter, being a wife, and as I did this, I began to appreciate my own mother and her journey a lot more. I began to understand what it took to be a parent, to be an independent woman in the midst of expectations of "normalcy". I began to see the way she survived before her illness and the way in which she allowed me to grow and grow strong as her daughter.

And, of course, just when I knew I would never appear as an actress again, let alone write another play, opportunity came knocking.

Here is the balance of the compelling reason. I was at a place where I was being forced to see the value in my everyday non-glamorous existence. I was "doing service" for a great many people. Everything from being a "pizza mom" at school, to being on the board of two theatres, to running two writers groups for free, to making sure the house ran smoothly, to being a helpmate to several sick friends.

My colleague called me and told me she had just lost a play for a series that was scheduled for production in a couple of months. Without the play, the evening could not go up. Did I know a playwright who had something we could use? How could I solve this problem? And it needed to be today, yesterday, immediately!

I had not one extra inch of space in my psyche for a telephone call or a search through old files for the perfect ten-minute piece that just happened to be about "hair", the theme of this multicultural evening.

I put my kid to bed, finished the dishes, walked the dog and sat down at my computer about 10 PM. In an hour, I had written HAIR: A REMINISCENCE . I just did not have time for the process to be difficult. It needed to be ready the next day. And the truth was I had been doing all the research and all the living and all the thinking that went into this simple little piece for the two years since I had written CLARICE. It has become one of my best pieces, I believe, and I will discuss this with you after you have had a chance to read it.

HAIR : A REMINISCENCE

> AT RISE: A PLUMP 60-ISH WOMAN DRESSED IN A SILK SHEATH AND BOUFFANT HAIRDO, SPIKE HEELS AND MINK STOLE OVER A PAIR OF OVERALLS. SHE SWAYS AS SHE SINGS SOULFULLY.

BETTY:

WHEN THE MOON IS IN THE 7TH HOUSE
AND JUPITER ALIGNS WITH MARS
THEN PEACE WILL RULE THE PLANETS
AND LUH-HA-HUV-HA–HUV WILL RULE THE STARS

SHE TOSSES AWAY HER STOLE
AND CONTINUES SINGING
WITH ABANDON.

THIS IS THE DAWNING OF THE AGE OF AQUARIUS,
THE AGE OF AQUARIUS.
AQUARIUS! AQUARIUS!

SHE TOSSES OFF HER SHOES
AND TURNS TO THE AUDIENCE

What? You think maybe I'll take the rest off like that Diana Keaton? Naw. Well, maybe later. She was stuffed underneath some canvas and in a lot of smoke anyway. Who knew, you know? I mean I know. I saw her. That night. In HAIR. That play? You remember?

Oy, I remember it like it was yesterday. I wore this very outfit. I wanted to look good. Look KOOL , like the kids would say. I mean I was always a mother who wanted to understand my children—or child in my case—but Linda had gone already, living in a van somewhere where it was hot with those mishuganeh boys with the beards like old rebbes. They looked like her zeyde.

I told her. I wasn't afraid. She was insulted. So. So, she didn't call after that for a long time.

But, that night—of HAIR—she was already gone. And Herb was as good as gone. Honestly, to think I would swallow that story that he couldn't drive home from Toledo and he had a discount coupon for a Holiday Inn anyway. What can I say? The world, it was a changing.

Anyway, I had these tickets and I was a subscriber and I'd had my hair done that day. And it was gorgeous. Mr. Emil had outdone himself. He did me himself which was a real honor and I had these damned tickets and I'd be damned if I was gonna stay home and sulk in my Spraynet.

So, I get into Herb's Cadillac, he'd taken the wagon on the road, easier to schlep his samples, and I drive right downtown to the Masonic Temple.

It is bitter cold in February, don't ask. But I have my stole from better days. And I have the caddy and my white leather gloves and I arrive... and yes, I am a bit overdressed for the crowd—but I take my seat in the theatre
not embarrassed to be myself, even in those years. And the lights go down and I tell you. I've never seen anything like it.

The children on the stage. The singing—shrying really—and all that hair—but then, of course—hence the title. And this sweet smell in the audience, smoky and I tell you I listen and I digest and I think and after awhile I just lose myself.

I think. This is new. This is something new. This is not Alfred Drake. Or Gordon McCrae. This is new and something about these unkempt children waiving their arms and flaunting themselves—I mean I recognize them I recognize my Linda.

I see her in front of that movie theatre—the Waverly—just like that girl on the stage and I think ; Oy vey, babeleh. Where are you now? Who ya lookin' for? I mean, Mamma's here, baby and here I am in the middle of watching that stage play HAIR and I am weeping like nobody's business.

It is foolish really but then, nobody notices. I mean, they are all doing what they are doing—eyes narrow—saying WOW every time the lights change. You know, appreciating life.

> SHE THINKS FOR A MOMENT
> AND THEN SOFTLY SINGS

HOW CAN PEOPLE BE SO HEARTLESS
 HOW CAN PEOPLE BE SO CRUEL
EASY TO BE HARD
EASY TO BE...

Well, I feel foolish, It is clear I do not belong here. I feel like some kind of sea creature, drenched in my tears, my mascara a wreck but—my hair solid. Well sprayed. Held beautifully in place by Mr. Emil's artistry. So, I make my way down the aisle, out of the theatre and I wait for my car in the windy parking lot.

I look up furtively, hoping I would see no one I know. But wouldn't you know it? There he is. There. Mr. Emil, there in the parking lot all alone, waiting for his car. He doesn't see me at first and I step back from view.

I actually don't recognize HIM, at first. A new toupee. He has a habit of changing them for special occasions and I like that about him. Always wanting to look good and always able to respond to the times. As he turns to get into his car his eye catches mine and well… he stops.

It is very moving Dear of him actually. He sees me. Probably recognizes that gorgeous bonnet he had built for me that day. The fall and all. And he pulls over and gets out of the car and he says: "Betty, Nice to see you, darling."

"Yes," I say.

"You're crying, Betty darling. The tears will freeze."

"Yes", I say.

And he says nothing. He simply, parks his car and takes my arm and steers me out of the parking lot and walks me through the cold February air. He holds my elbow and steers me round and round the block while my eyes leak liquid and he simply says:

"Yes, Betty darling. Yes, dear."

And the wind whips my face and freezes the fear back inside and then gradually our teeth start to chatter and we start to laugh and talk and say how cold we are, though both our heads are warm as toast. And we see a little White Tower nearby. We go in and I treat him to cocoa and a burger or two. They're so tiny! And I do. I begin to feel cozy and cared for and I squeeze his hand, just to thank him. And yes—there is a silence and smiles sweetly at me.

"Oh S-ss-sssweetheart, darling. It will be fine. Herb will come back and so will Linda. Just when you don't want them anymore. Take it from me, honey. Alone ain't always lonely, huh?"

And I think: Maybe you're right. And I say: "Maybe you can be my sweetheart," and start to pish again. And he takes my hand and says:
"All my girls are my sweethearts. You know that, huh?"
And I shake my head, sure, since I realize that his idea of a sweetheart and mine are a little different. But that is fine, because he is dear. Absolutely dear to me.

And we get through that moment and we both go home to our separate homes and I sleep well for a change and think and think and think about a change, maybe! A career in cosmetology, maybe and the joint is jumping inside my brain but not a hair of my head moves outside—naw—everything is safe and secure underneath Mr. Emil's grand construction. I can think. Make plans and preparations. And I am grateful to him for it. And I know I don't have to stay undercover forever.

Herb comes home a week later. I change the locks and take possession of the Caddy.

> BETTY REMOVES THE BOUFFANT WIG, HANGS UP THE STOLE, REMOVES THE DRESS. SHE IS WEARING OVERALLS AND HER HAIR IS LOOSE AND FREE.

Linda calls a few years after that. She is changed by this time. Really different. Maybe I am, too.

I meet her in a coffee shop downtown. She says she can't stay long. She looks tired. Really tired and there are actually streaks of grey in her hair. Herb has been sending her money, she says. Though he never gave me a penny. That is ok. I am working for Dottie Schwartz and Emil at the salon by now. Doing nails and feeling free. My hair is long and curly and I am only fifty.

She is do bedraggled and tired, my child. And I ask how she is and she can't sit still, like she has ants in her pants. And I tell her, I say,

"What's wrong, Linda?"

"Rainbow," she says.

"Rainbow. What's wrong? It's like you got ants in your pants."

"I'm nervous, ma. I'm just nervous."

"Oh," I say. "Don't be nervous. I'm still your ma, ain't I?"

And it's Linda's turn to cry. Her face just melts right in front of me. Her eyes drip and her nose slides half way down into her mouth.

And I pat her and say: "Yes, Linda, darling. Yes, my baby." Just like Mr. Emil did those few years ago for me.

And Linda hugs me and says: "I like your hair."

"Thanks," I say. "At least it's clean."

And that sets Linda off again and then I start too and I think the whole coffee shop is just gonna float away and then I say to my child.

"Did you ever see HAIR? The musical? I just kept thinking of you standing so forlorn in front of a movie theatre like that girl in the play and it made me so sad when I saw it."

"I don't like movies, Ma. I haven't seen one in years."

"Oh," I say, having no other response.

And then I take her grubby red hands and bring her back to the salon and Mr. Emil washes and blow dries her hair, a little highlight here or there, why not? And Dottie plucks her eyebrows and waxes her legs, ripping those follicles out right by the roots. It is good for her.

And then I do her nails and rub those hands till they are soft and young again and finally, I take another sneak peak into my baby's eyes and she is still there.

That night, my Linda sleeps in my bed for the first time in maybe twenty-five years. And her head lay on Herb's pillow and her hair sweeps the sheets and I can't keep from patting it, every last curl and highlight, all night long.

> SHE SINGS SOFTLY, LIKE A LULLABY.

WHEN THE MOON IS IN THE 7TH HOUSE
AND JUPITER ALIGNS WITH MARS
THEN PEACE WILL RULE THE PLANETS

AND LOV-HA HUV HA HUV WILL RULE THE STARS...

> SHE PICKS UP A HAIRBRUSH.
> SETTLES HERSELF ON A STOOL
> AND BRUSHES HER HAIR. SHE
> SIGHS.

Oy, Aquarius.

This little play has been done in many venues with many different kinds of audiences. It always succeeds and I have learned a great deal about writing and my self as a solo artist because of it.

This little play is very simple. The character, at first glance, seems a stereotypical Jewish woman with little depth. I grew up with people like this woman. Most of them were not hip, most were extremely aware of conformity and convention. They wore the same clothes from the same stores; they went to the same synagogues and were aware of the cars that their neighbors drove. Some were noveau riche and the ones who weren't, wanted to be. At first glance, they were dismissible. At least that is what I thought when I was growing up with them. Then, I grew up, looked again, and realized that each of these people was specific to who they were. Though they may appear to be outwardly the same, they each had a secret and a passion that drove them through their suburban lives. They struggled mightily for meaning and were idealistic in the best possible way.
They possessed a naiveté born of post war hope, but were making up the rules as they went along. These people, my parents' generation, were truly living in a brave new world.

I write very close to stereotype and like to play with this edge. I like to trick people into thinking that the people I put on the stage are nothing special, until you get to know them. I love to create a middle class Jewish businessperson like ERNIE who loses it and murders his wife. Or a frumpy housewife like BETTY who we think has no wisdom when it comes to the world and can be dismissed as a clown, until she is confronted with a daughter in desperate need of her help and she rises beautifully to the occasion. I find these every day "types" to be persons of weight and surprise and depth. This is the kind of person I hope I have created in BETTY.

This play is simple. If it's fully produced it needs a wig, a dress and a shawl. That's it.

> —There is one narrator, (BETTY).
> —There are three short movements:
>> 1: BETTY at the play, realizing that her old life had to change;
>> 2: BETTY making the change in her life by becoming a manicurist and taking responsibility for her own happiness and
>> 3: BETTY, having learned to love herself, able to give and receive love unconditionally.
> —There is an easily recognizable central character.
> —The play is filled out by commonly understood references to the issues of the time.
> —The theme of love, self-love, and unconditional love is universal and easy to understand.
> —There is humor. It doesn't take itself too seriously.

After all the twists and turns of CLARICE and the dark shadows flushed out by thick prose, this tiny little piece was the exact antidote. No muss, no fuss, just life.

This character came from a core of my true voice, mixed with my own experience of being both a mother and a daughter. It is simple and resonant, I believe, and I discovered a simplicity and clarity in this piece that I try to keep with me.

RECOGNIZING OUR TRUEST VOICE
As we continue our work as artists, especially generative artists, we begin to recognize patterns, themes and voices in our work. There are rhythmic repetitions that slide easily off our computer screens and onto our tongues. There are certain eras that come easily—certain styles and themes. We begin to recognize where our clearest voice can be heard and through what medium.

This is not to say that stretching is not important. Nor is it to say that we must always write the same thing from the same character, but if you look through your own work I am sure you will find these voices that keep returning to and through it. Voices that demand to be heard and addressed.

For me, the voice of BETTY, the voice of CLARICE, the voice of IDA in my play BEYOND THE SEA all have the same humor, the same wisdom, the same longing for love and completion. They are not such unusual characters but they are the truest characters that I have written. I recognize them deeply and can feel their every maneuver. They are truly true to me and I believe the audiences that have met them, see this truth and are able to understand and be moved by them. It is not because they are so brilliant. It is because they take care of themselves—they do the work they are supposed to do—so the audience can do theirs.

Because these characters are complete and full, there are no false beats to confuse an audience or force them to puzzle through the problem of who these people are. One can like them or not, but the fact that they are rendered clearly allows an audience to experience them and then sit back and digest their own experience in relation to the clear portrait before them.

It is easier to watch characters that are real because we needn't worry about them. We have room to have our own thoughts and responses to the characters and the situations they are in. We know the characters have a strong structure and life in which to live. The play is working, the characters fulfill their worlds and the audience is free to experience the play and their own personal reaction to it.

I am speaking here of characters rather than the 'I' as presented in an "autobiographical" solo play. I believe that audiences more easily interact with "characters" than with the naked 'I' of the autobiographical play. When a solo artist is just herself, not someone else, it can be more difficult for an audience to relax. In some ways, an audience feels responsible for a stand up performer with no "persona" to hide behind. They may feel the need to "be polite" to this person on the stage telling them about her life straight on with no filtering mask to protect both performer and audience member. The best solo "autobiographical" performers—people I admire like Eddie Izzard and Sandra Tsing Loh—still have a persona that represents their 'I'. It's them up there, but them within a secure framework and we have nothing to worry about.

In thinking about the kind of characters that I have, to date, written and created most successfully, I assumed that these people are simply another version of myself. Isn't it common wisdom that everyone we write is really ourselves wearing a different hat? I went back and looked at their common threads. I was startled to find that these characters are not me at all. They are my mother.

Oh man, I thought. Haven't I finished this one up in therapy? Haven't I done all the grieving and all the longing and all that messy stuff already? Haven't I, a mature woman in midlife, gotten over the fact that sometimes life is rough and there you are?

The answer is yes. Of course. But the journey of my mother's life has moved me more deeply than any other journey I have witnessed and for better or for worse I am constantly engaged in examining that journey and celebrating the parts of it that I fear will be lost.

I write my mom's humor, hope and despair. I write the many women she could have been if she had not been overcome by crippling depression. The loss of that vibrant spirit has become the single most significant experience in my life. Coming to terms with who she became has been a lifelong task. Coming to terms with who I have become—because of who she became—is the ongoing work.

Digesting the fate of a parent is a difficult process. No matter how much therapy one has, no matter how successful and wise we become on our own terms, we cannot escape the fact that for better or for worse we are our parent's children. Their successes affect ours and their failures haunt us.

I have a dear friend who recently told me that one of her earliest memories, as a child of maybe seven or eight, was to proudly figure out that if we just "could do without hope and vanquish fear", we'd be just fine. Can you imagine this statement coming from a seven or eight year old child? She laughed when she said this, recognizing that her load has been there from the earliest days of her life.

This friend is the child of concentration camp survivors. No matter how gay and delightful her life has been, no matter how loving or daring she has been, she is and always will be the child of people who had to forget about hope and live without fear if they were to get through the life that was left to them.

This discussion becomes relevant to us as writer/performers as it informs the choices that we make naturally and the roads we choose to avoid. To know your truest voice allows you to make some choices about it.

QUESTIONS TO PONDER;
> Are you aware of your truest voice?
> Does it limit you?
> Does it express your own passions?
> Does the voice speak from you or through you?
> How close is it to your own self? How far away? What do we learn about ourselves as we discover our truest voice?
> Does it truly express the most engaging issues that snag you as a writer?

LEGACY

In writing what we write and choosing projects to perform, we most often do what is in front of us, but as we move ahead and our basic stories are told, we might want to pause a moment and think about what comes next and why. What is the power of the words we write and the characters that we bring to life? Even if we do not become household words and strut across the many stages of the world, we still are creating words and people through whom the world gets to know our deepest passions. What do we really believe about the world? What kind of place is the world and how do we feel about its many faces, phases? Who do we channel and why? Why should anyone care to share our discoveries?

It does not inflate our worth to be cognizant of the fact that our work has an affect. It has an affect if no one ever reads it. If it is never published or performed.

We, as artists, doing our work every day one foot in front of the other, one word after the other, are creating energy that helps keep the world running. Just like gardeners and grocery clerks. Salespeople and bus drivers. Artists create and the world is in balance because of this fact. The energy travels.

We are witnesses to inner and outer actions. We witness and digest and eventually we recycle this witnessing. We observe the world and that observation can't help but enrich the life of others. Sometimes, all that means is that we are more able to share a joke with some stranger in the grocery line because we have opened ourselves to what his experience might be like. There is value to our work. There is benefit to our being.

If we are able to capture the lilt of another person's voice, or tell their story, we gain insights about ourselves in relation to that person and the rest of the world who share that lilt or live that story.

Everyone everywhere has basic needs. We need to eat, we need to love, we need to mate, and we need to grow. How we fulfill these needs or thwart their fulfillment is the story of our lives and this we all share. Do we need to tell our stories? Yes. But if we tell them to only a few others, we have still done the work of changing the energy, distilling the facts, understanding the nuance, distributing the power of the resolution—and that energy goes into the world one way or the other. Our work changes lives. Ours and other peoples. Empathy enriches the planet.

TO CREATE THE WORK
I have been lucky enough to be part of an ongoing writers workshop called the Los Angeles Writers Bloc. Emerging from the Writers Bloc in New York started by Jeffrey Sweet, Tony Shultz, Jane Anderson and I started the LA Bloc. The three of us knew that the New York Bloc, home to such writers as Percy Granger, Michael Wright, Jeffrey Sweet, Donald Margulies, Jerry Stiller and Anne Meara, had been an important touchstone of our New York lives. As we all moved west, we knew that we needed this same kind of group on the left coast. Meeting first in Jane Anderson's living room, the Bloc eventually moved to our living room and continues to meet every Monday night. We have been at it so far for nineteen years.

The group has morphed a bit over the years, people come and go with their own needs and talents, but it remains a place of safe haven where peers can gather to support each other and our work. The west coast members have included Janet Fitch (WHITE OLEANDER), Noni White and Bob Tzudiker (TARZAN, HUNCHBACK OF NOTRE DAME etc), Bostwick and Singer (MULAN), Irene Mecchi (LION KING) to name just a few. We have had marriages, and Emmy's and children and even death. We have seen it all over the years and we continue to meet and support each other and the work. I cannot stress enough the importance of finding such a home for you as an artist.

There is no magic formula to the Bloc except the willingness of everyone to say, "yes" first to every writer and their instincts. In this kind of 'safe haven', non-competitive environment, we believe that praise will push writers farther than crushing criticism. Because we have known and worked together for so many years, we have ease with each other and know each other's shortcuts and manipulations. We have a short hand and can get to the heart of the matter quickly with humor and history. New members marvel at the depth of criticism that can be dispensed with respect, kindness, encouragement and support.

The Bloc may be a special situation, but if you do not have such a group to work with, create one. This is the group that will help you to identify your truest voice and push you to expand that voice and grow to the next step.

## ELEMENTS OF THIS PLAY

ONE NARRATOR
An easily recognizable character who is specific to herself therefore avoiding cliché and illuminating a basic truth

SIMPLE STRUCTURE
Easy to follow movements of beginning, change and revelation.

USE THE TIMES TO STREAMLINE THE WORLD
With a few references to the external world of the character, the setting and tastes of the character are revealed without the need for much detail. Remember the idea that the energy of the external world of the character ignites with the character's inner world to create conflict and heat.

THE TRUEST VOICE
Writing simply from the truest voice gives a clarity and power to a seemingly simple story.

LEGACY
Without putting too much pressure on yourself, realize that this kind of simple clarity can be powerful in delineating your values and offering your solution to the pickle of human existence. Can it be that we have an opinion about how to survive? Maybe not, but the characters that speak with the truest voices certainly do.

**NOTES:**

Susan Merson as Clarice in CLARICE COHEN'S TRIBAL
TALES OF LOVE
Photo by Barbara Bloom

## VII: SOLO ESSENTIALS- A Shorthand to the Acting Elements Basic to Solo Performance

I have discussed six different approaches to creating your own solo play. No matter which style you choose, including styles that I have not covered, you will need some solid and strong acting tools to make the pieces live. Here is an overview of the technical acting skills that you'll need to hone when approaching solo performing.

PHYSICAL FITNESS
We start with the idea of physical presence. What do you look like onstage? Are you in control of that look? Are you able to sustain control of your body?
I am speaking not only of costume, but also rather of your physical instrument. Solo performing is taxing and you need to be physically fit and ready to make the work happen. So first, get into shape. That doesn't necessarily mean get thin. It means, get strong. Strong enough to look weak if you choose to appear so. Know that you are embarking on an aerobic activity and you need to be physically strong to do it. Walk every day, or swim or play tennis but move the major muscle groups and sweat. It's not enough to mean to do it. You need the stamina to proceed.

PHYSICAL FLEXIBILITY AND CONTROL
I recently saw the Berliner Ensemble perform Brecht's ARTURO UI. The lead actor chose to portray the Hitler character as a rabid dog and throughout the performance contorted his body constantly, throwing his legs up over his head, balancing on one hand and kicking out at his underlings, undulating in frustration and thwarted passion. The man was terrifying. The actor was brilliant. I was stunned at the way he maintained that physical choice and wondered how he could possibly sustain it. After the performance, I thought back and realized he was doing yoga asanas (poses) throughout the show but pushing from one to the other so quickly that the audience was not aware that

153

his physical choices had a form and method. With each asana, he was able to connect his own body with his character through the yoga pose. It looked like he was writhing as a dog might but instead he adapted his own yoga flow practice to serve him in this interpretation. It was brilliant and demonstrated a wonderful understanding of need for flexibility and control in performance. He put an edge on each pose so it appeared threatening but his movement was grounded in a body/mind discipline that held and supported him as he moved through the range of this madman. Not every interpretation will be so physically based, but this actor was in control of his choices.

In the same way, you need to be in control of the way your body telegraphs character and emotion. All movement comes from the belly, the core—and Pilates or yoga allows you to get in touch with your center and move from that strength. Alexander Technique also strengthens, refines and articulates your spine, which in turn supports you and the many people you are. Your physical body is your character's shorthand and you want to make sure that you are leading people in the right direction. Be in charge of your body and realize that gesture and physical tone tell us as much as voice and text.

Remember that Del Sartre developed an entire system of acting that had nothing to do with emotional recall as a first step. Instead, he told actors that where they placed their arms, their heads, their legs—the poses they struck, created a certain visual impression and that the emotion would follow the physical choice. It is an interesting discipline to recall in this age of interior acting styles designed for the small or large screen. You are on stage and you do not have the editor or lighting director focusing the audience for you. Your body commands the respect and focuses the audience's attention, so be ready.

GETTING IN SHAPE EMOTIONALLY
There are two aspects to getting in shape emotionally to do a solo play. One is the practical aspect. Be prepared for venues and sponsors that do not always understand your needs. It is easy to feel victimized by a booker who wants you to travel six hours, do a cue to cue tech rehearsal and then perform four shows in 24 hours and meet with audience members after each show—all for two dollars and a smile. This will happen.

Remember you are an educator and your job is to educate your audience and your presenter about what it takes emotionally, physically and financially to show up and get the job done well. Also, it helps to do your research and know where the nearest spa can be found. I make sure there is a line in my budget that reads 'personal' and which I reserve for a massage or facial, when needed, on the road!

The second aspect is to examine the emotional demands of your piece and decide two things. The first is how you will access emotional material and keep it real. How do you avoid the pitfalls of a technical performance? The second aspect is how to develop some personal tricks that will allow you to access the correct emotional depth for the piece in a consistent manner without wringing yourself out every performance. This should be part of your rehearsal process. Finding the way into a piece, finding the way to keep it fresh. One wants to maintain the "illusion of the first time" with every performance but this must be something that we can control consistently. Part of our physical readiness is to know where the emotional truth is sitting in our psyche. We need to put the access button for that truth into our toolbox and know how to activate it. Sometimes a physical gesture will take you right where you need to be. Work out these physical cues for emotional beats. We need our mind/body skills to keep us centered as our characters careen through their stage lives.

In the third act of VANITIES, a play I did over eight hundred times, I had flung my arm out across the audience like I was casting a fly like an angler. This gesture literally hooked my energy to the taxing structure of the rest of the play and allowed me to move through it night after night with ease and grace. Yes, there were times it didn't work and it was painfully obvious that I could not muster the "illusion of the first time" when it was performance seven hundred and three— but most times, the physical gesture helped me access the energy I needed.

In most cases, we will not have the luxury of a consecutive run of the piece so we need to find ways that we can quickly return to our emotional centers, even if we have not done the piece in a few days or weeks. These kinds of gestures can help us here too, to remind us physically of where we need to go as actors.

We lock the technique in during our rehearsal process and then, each performance did, what Meryl Streep calls "the shine", to give the material its special energy every night. The best material, consistently presented, still needs the "shine" of life from an actor. Find the reservoir of "fairy dust" that you can easily access and make each performance come alive.

## VOCAL READINESS

Train. Get your voice ready for speaking up to two hours, without stopping, every night. If you can't find a teacher in your area that works only with actors, then study with a singing teacher and learn the basics, allow these basics to become part of your body readiness. Always do vocal warm ups and always walk the performing space—stage and audience—allowing your voice to fill every corner of the room. Make sure you are respectful of your vocal chords and know how to produce a sound. Do sit ups and get your stomach and diaphragm strong. Remember people find it harder to hear someone when they can't see them and I guarantee you many a stage with lousy lighting.

Do old-fashioned tongue twisters and get your mouth and tongue moving to shape sound. How about: "Lips, teeth, tip of the tongue" or "red leather, yellow leather" or—my favorite, courtesy of Evangeline Machlin, my voice teacher at Boston University, many years ago, "In the lounge sat a dull frump on a binge". Say these fast and slow, in high register and low.

Know that the human voice has a resonant energy that affects a room. Think of those Buddhist monks and their throaty chants of OHM filling their monasteries every day and night. They are not only listening to the sound of their voices. They are feeling the sound of their voices. Learn to depend on the feel and resonance of your voice as another tool to support you as a solo performer. Find a Kundalini yoga class in your area and take it a few times. Learn how sound can affect physicality and the energy in a room.

Learn to trust the musicality of the words you are saying. The music of the text can help an audience understand what you are saying as much as an audience hearing and interpreting every word.

Learn your lines while doing a physical activity. If you are not actually doing your blocking every time you go over your words and say them out loud, then make sure you are doing some supportive physical movement as you talk. This will increase your stamina and allow you to speak while moving without running out of breath. It will also help you retain the words and their music. Movement helps the brain to learn. Movement will support your vocal energy. It will teach you how to relax your vocal instrument and respect its physicality. We forget that our voice boxes are part of our bodies. Remember. And get the voice in shape along with, and as part of, your physical training.

CONTROLLING THE ENERGY
Do you know about chakras yet? Chakras are those points in the body from which energy flows. That's a very basic and simple explanation and there is more to know. To be a solo performer on a stage one needs to know about the way in which energy comes and goes, how we contribute to it, drain it, gather it and distribute it. Yoga will help you to begin to understand prana—life force or life energy—and how it moves through and around you. As an actor, this is your most important tool.

I tell my students to go home and practice telekinesis. I am only half joking. It is necessary to know how to send your personal energy out into a space and fill it, soothe your audience or rile them with a look. I also like to invoke the spirit of Helena Blavatsky, one of the founders of the Theosophist movement. There is a great deal of controversy around this colorful figure, but indisputably, she had the ability to control a room. I know that I am writing in shorthand here, but I want this section to pique your interest and send you out to research these ideas and people on your own.

So, practice telekinesis. Expand your interior space to allow it to hold the command and control center of the room. The calibration system belongs right in your belly and the beams of light come out through your charkas.

Once you get in touch with the energy that you generate and control, you will also learn respect for it. There are times I have created a great deal of heat with a character and ended up burning my own fuses. When I appeared in Caryl Churchill's play TOP GIRLS, it was the only time in my career when I literally could not speak onstage. There was something about accessing the unfamiliar male energy that was necessary to play the role that I was not ready to integrate. It literally rendered me speechless.

The study of prana, energy and light is central to understanding "the shine" discussed in the previous section. Get in touch with your silence before you speak. Go within in order to support a strong and centered external energetic presence. Make sense? No joke. Get in touch with the hocus before you step out on stage so you can be the channel and not the victim of your own powerful work.

DEFINE CHARACTER THROUGH VOICE, ENERGY AND PHYSICALITY.

Delineate physically, with voice, focus and body. With a ready physical instrument and psyche, you need to practice definition of character in performance. Whenever you choose to voice more than one character—which is often in solo plays—it is necessary to define your voice as Narrator in contrast to the voice of the other character or characters in the scene. How do you do this? You do it physically, vocally and by changing the energetic field of the characters. This last requirement—the changing of the energetic field—follows naturally upon the physical definition of character.

The eyes have it in this area. Your eyes and their focus lead the audience. You direct the energy and focus with first; your eyes and then, you set the focus with a physical adjustment. You must do this swiftly and clearly. When you are juggling the definition of several characters at the same time, you bear the responsibility of making sure they are all created clearly and equally. Sometimes your eyes alone can make the shift, but don't count on it. Back up your energetic voice with physical adjustments and vocal specificity.

ACT BETTER/SMOKE BETTER

I received this note from director Garland Wright one night after a sloppy performance of VANITIES that earned my temperamental director's contempt. He simply wanted me to pull up my socks and do EVERYTHING better. I was devastated as a young actress. I didn't have a clue as to what action I could take to generally improve and sharpen my performance.

I eventually learned that it wasn't what I needed TO DO. Instead, it was what I needed NOT TO DO. I needed to go deeper, be simpler, be more connected and respectful of my material and believe it would support me. I needed to do nothing, and I needed to BE there a great deal more. Just show up fully—every part of me loose and active. This is the wonderful mystery and joy of acting. It is like trying to define a Zen koan. One needs to BE the moment, not ACT the moment. One needs to develop a deep understanding of that statement and practice.

Pay attention. Practice standing still and being present and absent. What is the difference in your attention? Is it centered inward or outward? How does that change your physical presence? Practice and observe life.

Look at fashion models still and in movement. Look at dancers. Look at real people. Steal and modulate the frequencies of their being. Cultivate the image of a button with which you can zap a focus, respond to that focus and create another person to whom, you offer your story.

## SELF CONFIDENCE

Here you are. You have made the decision to perform solo. You now must cultivate what the Zen masters call "right attitude". Consider the difference between a stand up comic and a solo performer. For me, the main difference is the commitment to "story" in the performance. A solo performer is there to embody and offer an entire story, an entire world. This is not about getting a laugh and dropping another set up for a joke. It is about creating a world and the characters that live in and against this world. So, "right attitude" is central to offering the story rather than your ego or your style. The more you connect with your material, the more you create the world that you are offering to the audience. This becomes even more central in the solo performing arena because you have no other actors to bounce off against. It's just you and the audience and they have to be willing to join you on your journey.

## ARE YOU REAL OR ARE YOU MEMOREX?

There was a marketing campaign some time back that showed the legendary singer Ella Fitzgerald in a recording studio singing live and then lip sync-ing what she had just put down on tape. The commercial was extolling the virtues of the then, fledging, digital computer industry. The question was, "Is it real or is it Memorex?"

On a recent film set, I was discussing the special effects with a technician who announced to me that I, as an actor, would be superfluous in a matter of years. "Now, we just bring the actor to a studio once, scan him into our computer and use his image to make a special effects sequence." He explained with a smirk that soon it would be common practice to use computer generated images, rather than actors, for all mainstream entertainment.

As I write this in 2004, the feature film POLAR EXPRESS is being readied for a Christmas release. The ads tout Tom Hanks as the star. If you look at the trailers, you do not see Tom Hanks. Instead you see a computer-generated image based on the features of the live person,

Tom Hanks. The image on the screen is a rubbery second fiddle to the real fellow. It has the same effect as PIXAR animation. That was interesting in TOY STORY and other films, though a bit soulless to this eye. But, at least, the process was generating characters from drawings. Here, we have the real actor's image obfuscated by technology. This kind of computer-generated image of actors is becoming more common. It saves a great deal of money for producers. But, is there a long-term affect? For actors, certainly. For the culture, probably so.

As artists, and live people, we must look at this question closely.

> QUESTIONS TO PONDER
> Does this technology enhance or limit our lives, our potential for creative solutions, and our personal power of imagination? How will we, how will you, weigh in on this technology as it affects you as an actor, a contributor to the cultural and spiritual life of your community?

AND THEN, THERE IS REALITY
Current programming on television features more and more "reality" programming. The trend started with the famous SURVIVIOR series and has grown to such an extent that a category has now been created for reality programming for the Emmy broadcast. Talk to anyone in the television business and they will tell you the enormous impact this form of programming has had on the employment picture across the industry. More importantly, there is an enormous cultural impact.

The thing about "reality" is that it is undeniably compelling. When you are actually watching the real AMERICAN IDOLs, or the Trump wannabes on THE APPRENTICE, it is very difficult to stay removed from their real plight. Will the young girls on AMERICA'S TOP MODEL survive the cut? Who will marry THE BACHELOR? How would it feel to have an EXTREME MAKEOVER? This is mainstream documentary film making which is affecting and directly related to the lives we live.

It is having an affect on our culture and its choices.

> QUESTIONS TO PONDER
> Why watch made up stories when we can eavesdrop on the real dramas on the making?

Why watch actors pretend to be in a crisis when the officers on COPS are really getting shot in front of us?

Why should viewers leave their television sets at all and hike to a local theatre to sit in the dark and watch you?

I am speaking about television here but since the media is so pervasive it sets the agenda for our cultural preferences. Think about this as you decide to enter the performance arena.

QUESTIONS TO PONDER

Why should people support you and your vision?

How will your humanity become compelling?

How will the stories you tell or interpret fit into this mainstream culture?

How does your solo work reflect or complement the mainstream culture?

Does it need to?

ACTING STYLES AND FANCY WORDS

Audiences weaned on television and used to movies may have a real problem with the "fake" theatricality of a play. Think about someone who has never seen a play who walks into a production of Oscar Wilde's IMPORTANCE OF BEING EARNEST. Are they going to recognize the people? Those strange accents? Weird clothes? Farcical, physical humor of Reverend Chausable? Lady Bracknell?

Is "naturalistic" kitchen style acting the only acting acceptable onstage for contemporary audiences? No. But with audiences that are less and less familiar with theatrical conventions, it means that you are required to commit and commit again to the style that you are using. The "truth" of the style will communicate to anyone who happens to come to the theatre whether educated or not.

You will have to convince the skeptical audience member that language is indeed understandable if it is not vernacular. If there is an essential and fierce truth to the character that is underlying all style and language choices, anything goes. But the truth rules.

BUT YOU STILL BELIEVE

It is common knowledge that theatre audiences are shrinking. Theatre producers are struggling valiantly against the wave, but it is a strong tide to pull against. There will always be live theatre, of course. It has been around since Thespis, so I doubt that we can totally obliterate the need for stories to pass from one live person to another BUT—

We must be aware that stories, storytelling and basic exchange of energy and ideas that we once took for granted is not an assumed plank in the foundation of the next generation. Children are not being regularly schooled in abstract thinking. They are being asked less frequently to sit quietly and engage with a simple, non-technological approach to their lives. So, if you embark on the artistic path, as an interpretative or generative artist, then you must take it as a real responsibility.

You must model the many layers of behavior and contradictions of soul that actors understand and can interpret. And your essential self is what makes the difference to the audience. You are the "constant" underneath all the characters that you create as a writer or an actor. In that "constant" energy, in that personal understanding and definition of the world from your point of view, lays the reason that the theatre will survive. You have a point of view that comes through when you tell the truth. We need that energy and point of view in the world.

Real people in reality or documentaries are important but they are not artists who come to their work with a quiet and solid point of view. An energy through which this point of view is channeled. This is compelling. This is why actors and the simple theatrical exchange are essential to our culture.

BELIEVE IN YOUR VOICE
Believe in your voice. Allow it to come from your passionate desire to speak, your practiced ability to voice your passion and your ongoing ability to listen. These three elements enable the solo performer to create worlds within worlds. Go. Open your heart and welcome us in.

"Look for your own.
And out of yourself create.
You are the most irreplaceable of beings."

**NOTES:**

# INDEX

————A————

ABOUT ANNE, 92, 93
Adaptation form, 71
       Elements of, 76
Affiliate Artists, 50, 52, 78
American Shakespeare Festival, 82
Anderson, Jane, 176, 146
Arnone, John, 18
Augustana College, 52
Autobiographical form, 17
       Elements of, 44

————B————

Bates, Kathy, 18, 79
Bletter, Diana K., 19

————C————

Cather, Willa, 73
CLARICE COHEN'S TRIBAL TALES OF LOVE, 109
       Opening monologue, 111
       Estelle monologue, 121
Cobb, Lee J., 18
Cohen, Edward M., 75, 81
Colette, 58, 73
Compilation form, 49
       Elements of, 66
Cooper, Paul, 29, 79
Cubiculo Theatre, 79

————D————

Dempster, Curt, 18, 119
DREAM ADJUSTMENTS, 55
       Lois Mitchell 52, 53, 55

**Susan Merson now** lives in Los Angeles after 17 years in the New York theatre where she appeared on, off, and off off Broadway in such plays as CHILDREN OF A LESSER GOD, the original company of VANITIES and the Zefirelli production of SATURDAY, SUNDAY, MONDAY. Since moving to LA, she has appeared in numerous television shows, plays and films casts including LOST IN YONKERS, PHENOMENON, TERMINATOR 3, and the upcoming PRIZEWINNER OF DEFIANCE OHIO with Julianne Moore.

Involved as actress/writer with new plays and playwrights since the early 70's, she has eight solo pieces to her credit as writer/ performer. She won a Best Actress Award in 1999 in performance with colleague Sherry Glaser's solo piece, FAMILY SECRETS.

Susan has served as the Producing Director of the Jewish Women's Theatre Project, (she is currently Resident Playwright), Artistic Director of the Streisand Festival, Associate Producer at the Fountain Theatre and co-founder and chief moderator (19 years) of the LA Writers Bloc, established with award winning writers Jane Anderson ( EMMY, HUMANITAS) and Donald Margulies ( PULITZER). Susan received her MFA in Creative Writing from Goddard College in Vermont.

Her fiction has been published in NICE JEWISH GIRLS, edited by Marlene Marks, Penguin; JEWS IN AMERICA, Hugh Lauter Levin; Lilith Magazine and GINOSKO. She also wrote the BACKSTAGE WEST book review column for two years, reviewing books on theatre and film.

Please visit her website at: http://www.susanmerson.com

Back Cover Author Photo by Lesley Bohm

# PLAYS/SCREENPLAY AND FICTION
# BY SUSAN MERSON
# LEARN MORE AT INFO@SUSANMERSON.COM

**ONE ACTS:**

MEETING BETTY SUE
After 16 years mother and birthmother meet again. Drama.

STAR TRAIN
Young widow meets elderly gent on train going west. Drama.

HOPE
A born-again Christian policeman on the way to an abortion clinic confronts a mother and daughter. Drama.

SARA'S LAST DANCE
A passionate affair leads a seventy-year-old man to murder. Drama.

DANSE RUSSE
When a young woman comes up missing, the patrician head of a Midwestern college is forced to confront her feelings for the girl and the man she has controlled for many years. Drama.

HAIR: REMINISCENCE
A solo play about a mama coming of age along with her hippie daughter. Comic drama Commissioned by the Jewish Women's Theatre Project, Jan Lewis, Artistic Director

ON THE WAY UP
A solo play spanning 25 years, about growing up in the theatre. Drama

**FULL LENGTHS:**

FIREWORKS OVER THE BACON
After many years, a woman comes to terms with the memory of her old lover. Comedy

BEYOND THE SEA
1966, Vegas and Bobby Darin is at the Riviera. A Midwestern family travels to Sin City finding love, lust and satisfaction. Comedy.

WHAT REMAINS
Based on the true story of a murder of a rabbi in front of his congregation in 1966. A play about love and violence commissioned by the Jewish Women's Theatre Project, Jan Lewis, Artistic Director. Drama

BOUNTY OF LACE
A romance between an Orthodox Israeli girl and an Arab boy leads to his death and her acceptance of the world at war. Commissioned by the Jewish Women's Theatre Project, Jan Lewis, Artistic Director. Drama

## FULL LENGTH SOLO PLAYS:

REFLECTIONS OF A CHINA DOLL
Coming of age story of young Jewish girl into womanhood.

THE LOVES OF SHIRLEY ABRAMOWITZ
A loose adaptation of Grace Paley's short stories. Wth Edward M. Cohen.

PICNIC IN EDEN
A poetry play about loss of innocence.

CLARICE COHEN'S TRIBAL TALES OF LOVE
A born again, sixty something chanteuse finds meaning in becoming the hit of the nursing home entertainment circuit. Comedy/drama.

## SCREENPLAYS:

MEETING BETTY SUE
A birthmother and mother meet again after 16 years.

DREAM DATE
Midlife marriage, affairs and finding each other again. Romantic Comedy

SWIMMING UPSTREAM
Eighteen-year-old Sam Silver moves to Beverly Hills to work at her uncle's beauty salon in 1963, to find her heroine, Esther Williams, and get on with her life. Comedy/Drama

## FICTION:

"Blood in the Sand", NICE JEWISH GIRLS, edited by Marlene Adler Marks.
Dutton /Plume Press

"Chicken Noodle Nightflights". Lilith Magazine

"Seclusion", Ginosko Literary Journal, Fairfax, California

## COLUMNS:

BACKSTAGE WEST: Book reviews

## Other Books By Star Publish

*The Frugal Book Promoter: How To Do What Your Publisher Won't*
**By Carolyn Howard-Johnson**
**Non-Fiction**
Whether your publisher assigns zero dollars to your book's promotional campaign or thousands, THE FRUGAL BOOK PROMOTER assures it the best possible start in life.

*Desert Heat: Affairs of the Heart*
**By Kristie Leigh Maguire**
**Ultra-Sensual Romance**
From the scorching sun of the Mojave Desert to the brilliant neon lights of Las Vegas, the sexy steel magnolia Marcie Treyhorne blazes a trail of passion through the desert sands.

*Battleground USA3: Lake Pepin*
**By Mark Haeuser**
**Action/Adventure**
As the Russian army moved in unopposed and the death toll mounted, the people of the area turned their pleas to the only group capable of helping: The West Central Wisconsin Commandos.

*Highway Hypodermics: Your Road Map to Travel Nursing*
**By Epstein LaRue**
**Non-Fiction**
As the nursing shortages grow, so does the popularity of travel nursing. So many nurses have so many questions. Don't take a shot in the dark down the highway of travel nursing. Find your answers in this book.

*The Rock of Realm*
**By Lea Schizas**
**YA Fantasy**
A thrilling action packed adventure that also teaches about discovery, friendship, and courage with the underlying moral theme that "all is not as it appears to be".

*Pilgrim Girl: Diary and Recipes from her first year in the New World*
**By Jule Selbo and Laura Peters**
**Historical Fiction**
Constance, a twelve year old girl, crosses the Atlantic on the Mayflower. Read the diary of her first year in the New World. Included are recipes of the food they prepared.

*Cabin Fever: Affairs of the Heart*
**By Kristie Leigh Maguire**
**Ultra-Sensual Romance**
Marcie Treyhorne leaves behind the blistering heat of the desert but the searing passion she carries with her to the northern Nevada mountains will melt the deepest of winter snows.

Printed in the United States
64162LVS00008B/30